TRUTH, LOVE, NON-VIOLENCE

THE STORY OF GURCHARAN SINGH BHATIA

TRUTH, LOVE, NON-VIOLENCE

THE STORY OF GURCHARAN SINGH BHATIA

ALEXIS KIENLEN

ISBN: 1493744046

ISBN 13: 9781493744046

Dedicated to all people who support human rights

TABLE OF CONTENTS

ACKNOWLEDGMENTS

This project would not have been possible without the time, effort and dedication of Gurcharan Singh Bhatia. I learned a great deal from him, and I am very grateful.

Gurcharan offered generous access to his personal archives and other resources. Jiti Bhatia welcomed me into the Bhatia home and filled in details of the story. The Bhatia family was always warm and welcoming to me, and I have enjoyed my time with them. Special thanks to Priti, Michael, Sam, Gurvinder and Aimee.

This book would never have been completed without the wise guidance of Linda Goyette. Thank you for all your time, effort, support and advice. You have helped me to become a better writer and editor by answering my questions and keeping me on track. Satya Das offered words of wisdom and gave me a variety of resources that helped with this project.

Dr. David Mills and Dr. Paul Voisey, history professors at the University of Alberta, helped me to understand what was happening in Canada in the 1980s and 1990s. I conducted numerous interviews during the writing of this book. Gurcharan's friends and associates were all generous with their time and thoughts. I would like to thank Marc Arnal, Jim Edwards, Karen Faulkner, Gerald and Karen Gall,

Jim Gurnett, Randy Gurlock, Doug Johnston, Wendy Kinsella, Paula Kirman, Robinson Koipillai, Zaheer Lakhani, Anne McLellan, Jack O'Neill, Radha and Sharma Padmanabhan, Karina Pillay-Kinnee, Indira Puri, Douglas Roche, Allan Sheppard, Amarjeet Sohi and Max Yalden.

I am also grateful to the staff at Citizenship and Immigration Canada, Edmonton branch, and to the staff at NorQuest College.

Two kind souls passed away while I was writing the book. I offer condolences to the families of Gerald Gall and Doug Johnston, both of whom helped me in my research.

My mother, Doreen Kienlen, encouraged me during all stages of this project. Cliff Kienlen offered a sympathetic ear. I am also grateful to Mari Sasano, Caitlin Crawshaw, Nathan Smith and Elizabeth Withey who listened to me talk though the intricacies of this book and offered helpful suggestions and distractions when they were needed.

A portion of the proceeds from the sale of this book will go to support the Daughters Day Initiative. To learn more about Daughters Day, please see www.daughters-day.com

To learn more about me, please go to www.alexiskienlen.com. To contact me directly, please email me at alexiskienlen@hotmail.com

ONE CHILD, A PROLOGUE

Gurcharan Singh Bhatia glimpsed the toddler amid the corpses ly-
ing on the street. It was 1947 in Jammu, during a period of intense
communal violence. Was the girl breathing? The girl, not two years
old, looked up at him with terrified eyes. Her family members lay dead
all around her, the Muslim victims of intense communal violence that
gripped the region. The Sikh teenager scooped the surviving child into
his arms. Walking quickly homeward, his young friends around him,
Gurcharan held on to the trembling girl as if she were the most important person in the world. In that terrible hour, her life was all that mat-
tered to him.

He reached the entrance of the home he shared with his mother and
his three siblings. His mother heard his call. Rushing toward him, she
reached out her arms to hold the child, dreading what would surely happen by nightfall, but knowing that her family had to protect the innocent
girl.

Gurcharan's immediate family members had already suffered the
terror, the riots, the massacres and the wrenching grief of personal loss.
Still, they believed in peace, helping others and the rejection of violence

during India's most frightening days and nights. Caring for the young stranger that day, the Sikh family waited for the worst—and then it happened.

Suddenly they heard pounding on the door and furious shouts on the street. A Hindu mob had discovered that Gurcharan had saved the girl, and they would not stand for it. Strangers shouted for the surrender of the child. The mob's fervour and hatred of Muslims was so strong that Kulwant knew they would kill the toddler if given a moment to do so.

A recent widow, she drew on every remaining shred of her personal strength, conviction and courage. She took a deep breath and opened the door. Facing the crowd, she found her voice.

"There is no child here," she said. "You are mistaken."

Repeating her words firmly, she was able to convince the mob to go away. Her son knew the family would have to act quickly before the crowd returned in an even angrier mood. That night, Gurcharan contacted his lifelong friends, Balraj Puri and Ved Bhasin, who had many contacts among the Muslim families in the area. Balraj, Gurcharan and Ved knocked on doors until they were able to find a family willing to protect the child. Risking their own lives, the boys took the girl to a safe haven.

Gurcharan Singh Bhatia is an old man now. Looking back, he describes his family's effort to save a single child as one of the most significant events of his life, a moment in time that shaped his future and strengthened his determination. He has devoted his life to the values of tolerance, compassion and human rights with small actions that have helped to make the world better for others. One small girl, clutching his strong shoulders with her tiny hands, gave him an early glimpse of his life's purpose.

INDIA

Forgiveness is the virtue of the brave.

~ MAHATMA GANDHI

CHAPTER 1

BEGINNINGS

Gurcharan Singh Bhatia was born at a time when India was at a crossroads, shaking off the shackles of Britain's colonial reign. The movement to eject the British from India had begun long before Gurcharan's birth. He came into the world on August 2, 1931 in the small city of Doraha, in the northern area of Punjab, a key region during the years of fighting after the partition of India in 1947.

Gurcharan spent most of his childhood in Jammu, a small market town of forty thousand people in the province of Jammu and Kashmir, located next to the Punjab. This area had always been a special area of India, an agricultural jewel nestled in the Himalayan mountain ranges. Prior to the partition, Buddhists, Muslims, Sikhs, and a Hindu majority lived together peacefully in the area. Jammu and Kashmir province is on the northern outskirts of India, bordering Afghanistan, China and Pakistan. Its position has long influenced the culture and politics of the region. Throughout the centuries, rulers from various countries sought to obtain this vital access point, a gateway to India herself. A prime recruiting ground for soldiers for the British army, the Punjab was a cultured area, home to a large middle class and the beautiful twin cities of Amritsar and Lahore. The Punjab is the birthplace of Sikhism.

Gurcharan was the oldest of four children. He was followed by his two sisters, Surinder and Kuldip, and brother Manjit. Surinder was two years younger than Gurcharan, Kuldip four years younger and Manjit eight years younger.

His mother, Kulwant Kaur Bhatia, had a Grade Eight education, considered typical for a housewife in Kashmir in the period. She was a deeply spiritual woman, interested in the world around her, and highly inspired by Gandhian principles and political events in India. She believed in God, strong family ties and the importance of education, values she passed on to her children. She was a tolerant person who did not believe in violence against other people. She and her husband tried to educate their children about the importance of doing good work, and acting fairly.

Gurcharan's father, Ishar Singh Bhatia, was the superintendent of police. Prior to being superintendent, he had worked as public prosecutor. Ishar earned a good income and could afford to build a comfortable house for his family in Jammu, the location of his first posting. The Bhatia home had three bedrooms, a living room, kitchen and bathroom. The house had outdoor toilets in the corner of the lot. The Bhatias had access to running water and electricity, but no sewage system, telephone or television.

The young family lived on Karanagar Street in a typical new development inside an area known as Rehari. The neighbourhood was filled with back-to-back houses, including an area where the Harijans, or lower caste Hindus, lived. Most of the population was Hindu, but Muslims and Sikh families like Gurcharan's also lived in the area.

Sikhism is a monotheistic religion founded in fifteenth century Punjab by Guru Nanak Dev. Most of India's Sikhs live in the Punjab, although a large Sikh diaspora has spread throughout India and to countries beyond, such as Canada, the United States and England.

Sikhs believe in the equality of all human beings and do not believe in discrimination based on caste or gender. Some think the religion may have been created as an offshoot of Hinduism, and as response to the caste system. Guru Nanak was the first to teach Sikh philosophy, and the nine gurus who followed after him built on his initial philosophy. Sikhism teaches that God is genderless, omnipresent and visible to the spiritually awakened. Heaven and hell do not exist; those who are en-lightened have a spiritual union with the divine. Sikhs believe in balanc-ing work, worship, service and charity, and they defend the rights of all living creatures, human beings in particular. Sharing is another crucial concept, exemplified through free, communal meals at Sikh temples, known as *gurdwaras*. Sikhs have adopted a number of cultural symbols and beliefs that they pass on to each successive generation. Each bap-tized Sikh man takes on the name *Singh,* meaning "lion," while baptized women are given the name *Kaur,* which means "princess." Sikhs fought against racism and the forced conversion of Hindus and other non-Mus-lims to Islam. The fifth guru, Arjun Deve, sacrificed his life fighting against Mogul kings. Guru Gobind Singh, the tenth guru, witnessed the sacrifices of his four sons and his father the ninth guru, Teg Bahadur, who lost their lives fighting against forced conversion to Islam. Guru Gobind Singh had many followers throughout the country during a time of militancy against Muslim rule. Later, the Sikh ruler, Maharaja Ranjit Singh promoted Sikhism as the state religion of the Punjab. The Sikh empire eventually participated in the Anglo-Sikh wars, before the em-pire fell under British rule.

Mohandas Gandhi, later known as the Mahatma, meaning a holy person, was one of the influential leaders who advocated for freedom from British rule. Gandhi was against partition and believed in a united India without separation or divisions. A Hindu by birth, he believed in pluralism and a country where people of different ethnic backgrounds and religions could live together. In one speech, he even indicated that the rest of India should look to Kashmir as a model for humanity, since Hindus, Muslims, Sikhs and Buddhists lived in the area peacefully. During his lifetime, Gandhi inspired many of India's four hundred mil-lion people, including the Bhatia family.

The Amritsar massacre deepened the resentment of many Indians toward the British. This was a pivotal incident that advanced the "Quit India" movement. On April 10, 1919, police arrested two Indians who had organized *hartals,* days of prayer and general strikes. People rioted in response to the arrest; forty thousand people ran through the city of Amritsar, burning buildings, pillaging shops, injuring two women and killing five white men. In response, Brigadier General Reginald Dyer arrived to take control of the situation. Dyer had previously enjoyed a good reputation and maintained control of his Indian soldiers. However, after the riots and injuries, he ordered his army to keep peace by firing on any mass gatherings.

On April 13, 1919, Sikhs and Hindus gathered to celebrate a festival known as Baisakhi day. Dyer ordered the public to refrain from gathering, but no one heard him. Later that day, Dyer received a report that a meeting was taking place in an enclosed area known as Jallianwala Bagh. People congregated to talk and celebrate with out-of-town relatives who had arrived specifically for the festival. A small political meeting occupied a corner of the square, an area with only two narrow exits. More than 140 armed soldiers arrived to watch the crowd. The general ordered his soldiers to march in and fire their rifles at the masses, picking up anyone trying to escape.

The peaceful gathering turned to chaos, and soldiers fired more than 1,650 bullets into a crowd of women, men and children. The panicked crowd tried to run to the exits but found them blocked by soldiers. Terrified festival goers tried to climb the walls to escape. The eventual death toll was unknown, with official reports putting the toll at 379 with at least 1,650 injuries. Reports from eyewitnesses estimated the casualties as much higher. Dyer showed no remorse for his actions. Instead, he rounded up high-caste Indians suspected of political activities and had them beaten in public. The Amritsar massacre agitated many Indians and made them passionate about the prospect of a free India. However, some Indians supported Dyer's actions and said he had prevented a mutiny.

***

Political parties and key individuals from India and England influenced Britain's decision to leave India. The Indian National Congress, a political party created in 1885, actively advocated for India's freedom. After the 1920s, the party transformed from a small party to a nationalist party with more than four million members. Another major political party, the Muslim League, formed in 1909 but didn't gain popularity until the Second World War. By the 1940s, both political groups were pushing Britain for a free India. Each had a different vision of the way India should look after independence. The Muslim League wanted a separate state for Muslims, while Indian National Congress desired a secular, united, multicultural and multinational India for all Indians.

Britain had many reasons to abandon India. The postwar economic situation in England was poor, and England was losing superpower status. Four of England's former colonies, the United States, Australia, New Zealand and Canada, had long since gained independence.

The Quit India movement worked for self-rule for many years. Leaders such as Jawaharlal Nehru, president of the Indian National Congress, and Muhammad Ali Jinnah, leader of the All-India Muslim League, led the nation's call for independence. Lord Mountbatten, England's last viceroy in India, also played an important role in the historic transition. In the years leading up to the 1947 partition, sporadic riots, mutinies and violent incidents occurred all over the country.

The nature of India itself presented a challenge. The country was divided into regions, but different princes controlled more than six hundred principalities throughout the country. India was home to many different ethnic groups, languages, religions and sects within religions. No one knew what would happen when India became free of her colonizer. There wasn't a soul who could have predicted the bloodshed and social unrest ahead—certainly not a young student in northern India with a passion for peace and human rights.

CHAPTER 2

THE INDEPENDENCE ACTIVIST

Gurcharan spent his childhood and early years in Jammu. By the age of thirteen, he was politically active and fascinated with regional and national events. It was hard not to be interested as everyone around him could sense that independence was on its way. Gurcharan first learned about the freedom movement at student meetings at his school. He joined the students' union along with his friends Balraj Puri and Ved Bhasin, young student leaders who remained Gurcharan's friends for life. The popular leader of Jammu and Kashmir, Sheikh Abdullah, President of the National Conference, was devoted to the Gandhian principles and secular "Free India" movement. He wanted to abolish the princely head of state Maharaja Hari Singh, and replace him with a popular government with an elected assembly. Abdullah wanted the Maharajah to surrender his political power and become a ceremonial head of the state. At that time, Jammu and Kashmir state was divided into three regions. The majority of people in Jammu were Hindus, while Kashmir was populated by Muslims, and Buddhists lived in Ladakh. Abdullah embraced secularism and was close to the Indian National Congress as it spearheaded the freedom movement in India.

Gurcharan would later speak about aspects of the independence struggle that intrigued him. "It was not politics, basically, it was the freedom movement and getting rid of imperialism, achieving freedom from the monarchy and the prince and getting democracy," he said. "At that time, Marxists were very active and we didn't realize the difference between Marxists and communists. We thought they wanted to help the poor and would stand up to help poor people. There was a lot of literature floating around in those days. We were fed a lot of free literature."

Gurcharan, like many of his classmates in the student movement, devoured the literature and entered the discussions. Gurcharan's mother spoke very little about the freedom movement, but Gandhi's speeches and appearances affected her. She believed Gandhi's views made sense and that he was the voice of reason. She was not politically active because she was busy taking care of her four children and maintaining the home, largely without the help of her husband, who spent most of 1947 and 1948 working a day's journey away in Mirpur, a city near the border.

Even though Gurcharan's father was stationed in Mirpur for two years and spent days away from the family, his actions had a major impact on Gurcharan's way of thinking and his ideals. Ishar Singh Bhatia wrote on letterhead inscribed, "Truth is God and God is truth." He lived life by that precept as one of the most honest officers in a police force prone to corruption. He received medals and high honours for his work. Gurcharan remembers two examples where other policemen acted in ways that were unjust and corrupt while his father took action to redress crimes committed by the police. The first incident happened on a Sunday. A crying shopkeeper knocked on the door of the Bhatia home and told Ishar his store had been robbed. The shopkeeper had already gone to the police station to report the crime. Since the police stations were located in open areas, the man had been able to look into the building at the sleeping officers. He had seen a tin of butter and a bag of sugar, products he carried in his store, under a police officer's bed. He came to Ishar for help.

"I could see my stuff," he said to Ishar. "If I told him that was my stuff, he could put me in jail for false allegations. So I come to you, because you are his superior. Those officers are corrupt."

Gurcharan's father listened closely, investigated further and went to the police station to suspend the corrupt officer. The stolen goods were returned to the shopkeeper.

In the second case, a man complained to Ishar about the corruption of an assistant inspector of police. Gurcharan's father learned the officer had taken one hundred rupees from the victim, so he went to the assistant police inspector's house to talk to him. He spoke to the assistant inspector's wife and asked her if she knew anything about the missing money. She gave him the hundred rupees, confessing her husband had brought the rupees home earlier that day. Ishar returned the money to the victim and the assistant police inspector was suspended.

Gurcharan's father wanted the police to be solid, honest and fair. He worked hard to make sure the police were law-abiding citizens, and his four children and wife were proud of his values and remembered his actions. Sometimes people asked Ishar why he didn't use his position of power for personal benefit but he always replied that he had enough money and was satisfied with his life. He had an abiding love for his family as well as dedication to his duties. By 1945, Ishar was stationed in Mirpur and visited his family in Jammu about three or four days a month. Gurcharan's extended family members, including his paternal grandparents, aunts and uncles, lived in Mirpur. There was no road between the two cities, so travellers had to travel to a city named Jhelum by bus or train, and then cross the Jhelum river by boat before arriving in Mirpur.

Gurcharan's strong sense of duty and honour developed because of his place in the family. As the oldest Sikh son, he was expected to help his mother look after his siblings and act as a successor to his father. He had always known he had to make a contribution to the family, study hard, obtain an education and do the best he could. Gurcharan's father also told him to take care of the family during his absence, and Gurcharan never forgot those words.

"I remember that once he came home and told me I was doing a good job. He bought me a new silk pyjama suit in recognition," said Gurcharan. He would have been about fourteen or fifteen years old at the time. Gurcharan's life was busy. He worked with the student movement, took care of his family, and spent the rest of his time learning and studying. He was especially interested in the words and actions of Gandhi, one of his lifelong human rights heroes and role models.

꧁꧂

Mohandas Gandhi's moral courage became an inspiration and a guide for the Indian people who wanted independence. His core principles were non-violence and truth. Indians acknowledged him as one of the leaders of their struggle for freedom from British rule. He published a weekly magazine called *Harijan* (Untouchable). Gurcharan was a regular reader of this publication and he listened to all of Gandhi's speeches and read all of his writing, as did many other Indians of this era.

A Hindu born in 1869, Gandhi grew up in the coastal state of Gujarat and earned a law degree in London before beginning his legal career in South Africa. He was a defender of the British Empire until the 1920s when he decided to advocate for Indian self-rule. While working abroad, Gandhi experienced racial prejudice, and by exploring the injustices around him through talking with others and reading, he began to develop his philosophy of non-violent resistance. He used this philosophy to organize the Indian community in South Africa to oppose race-based laws and discrimination, and adopted non-violent resistance as a method to use in India when he returned home in 1914. By 1929, Gandhi had reshaped the Indian National Congress to promote Indian self-rule; participants in the Congress actively embraced the goal of Indian national independence.

Gandhi's principles of non-violence emerged from his spiritual beliefs. He opposed the use of force of any kind and believed violence was never the correct path to take. Any violent act resulted in more violent acts, he said. Gandhi said embracing non-violence was courageous, the higher moral choice, and his ideas spread throughout India and the world. Many great leaders, including Martin Luther King, Jr., Nelson Mandela and Desmond Tutu, studied his works and philosophy, and added them to their own. Gandhi concerned himself with the lives of the less fortunate: the downtrodden, oppressed and the poorest of the poor. He opposed child marriage, the concept of an "untouchable" caste, and the oppression of Hindu widows, including the practice of *sati*, when widows threw themselves into the funeral pyre. Women could participate as equal citizens in all of his campaigns, an unprecedented practice in India.

He led nationwide campaigns to alleviate poverty, expand rights for women and increase economic self-reliance for the Indian people. He did not believe any one ethnic or religious group should control India but worked to unite people of all backgrounds. However, India did not always listen to Gandhi's message. Throughout the independence movement, shootings and other violent incidents occurred at railway stations, telegraph offices, government buildings and public institutions across the country. Famines afflicted various regions across the subcontinent, including Bengal. Under British rule, Indians were not free to develop their own industries and resources. Many people, including Gurcharan's father, Ishar, rightly suspected the political situation would deteriorate in the country before it improved.

Gandhi's role was to encourage Indians to act. He did this by attempting to stage peaceful protests, and he gave speeches to encourage people to follow his teachings. He began to use the principles of non-cooperation, non-violence and resistance against the British Raj. He led a national protest against the Amritsar massacre, criticizing both the actions of the British as well as the violence of Indians. He offered sympathies for the deaths of British civilians at the same time as he began to advocate for Indian self-rule and self-government. His focus on *swaraj,* or Indian self-rule, emphasized throwing off the shackles of British political, economic, legal, military, and educational institutions. In 1920, he reorganized the Congress with a new constitution and opened the membership in the party to everyone. His strength of character and his popularity amongst diverse groups of Indians solidified his leadership. He expanded his platform to include a *swadeshi* policy, a boycott of foreign-made products - especially British goods. He wanted people to spend time each day spinning *khadi*, homespun cloth for clothes, in support of the independence movement, effectively eschewing British textiles. He urged people to boycott British educational institutions and law courts, to resign from government employment and to forsake British titles. During his lifetime, he was arrested twelve times and imprisoned multiple times following his arrests. On several occasions, he gained popular support for his movement through self-imposed hunger strikes.

In 1928, he pushed through a resolution at the Calcutta Congress calling on the British government to grant India dominion status. He announced a campaign of non-cooperation until independence was granted. The British did not respond to his call, so he pushed on with other non-violent actions. One of Gandhi's most successful acts of peaceful protest was the salt march he undertook in March 1930. He symbolically rejected the economic authority of the British by walking 388 kilometres from Ahmedabad to Dandi in Gujarat to collect salt from the sea. Thousands of people marched with him. Britain responded to the mass action by imprisoning sixty thousand people.

Gandhi opposed India's involvement in the Second World War and continued to agitate for independence. On August 8, 1942, he delivered his famous Quit India speech at Gowaliar Tank Maidan in Bombay. In one part of the speech, he called the people of India to action while continuing to advocate equality, non-violence and democracy:

> Ours is not a drive for power, but purely a non-violent fight for India's independence. In a violent struggle, a successful general has been often known to affect a military coup and to set up a dictatorship. But under the Congress scheme of things, essentially non-violent as it is, there can be no room for dictatorship. A non-violent soldier of freedom will covet nothing for himself; he fights only for the freedom of his country. The Congress is unconcerned as to who will rule, when freedom is attained. The power, when it comes, will belong to the people of India, and it will be for them to decide to whom it placed in the entrusted.

Gandhi's full speech galvanized Indians in the independence movement in much the same way as Martin Luther King Jr. would later inspire a different generation of Americans when he spoke of his dream of racial equality in the United States.

Gandhi was arrested the day after his speech and held for two years in the Aga Khan Palace in Pune until he was released for medical reasons. Throughout his campaigns, he opposed the partition of India because it offended his vision of religious harmony and national unity. He suggested that the Muslim League and Congress work together to create one nation, but the Muslim League still wanted to create an independent Muslim nation, separate from secular India.

Gandhi believed that peaceful existence among all types of people was possible. In one speech, he talked about the history of Kashmir, a place where people of different faiths had co-existed without violence for hundreds of years. The peace in this area was soon to become a distant memory, as the area was divided between two warring nations, and many innocents, like the Bhatia family, suffered during the following years. Gurcharan greatly admired Gandhi's actions and has always embraced the Gandhian philosophy. Gandhi's ideas and the principles of truth, justice and non-violence would continue to play a great role in Gurcharan's life.

CHAPTER 3

DAYS OF GRIEF
AND LOSS

While Gandhi and other Indian political leaders met for difficult negotiations, trying to resolve India's independence struggle, Gurcharan was doing his part to help the movement at home. "There was a feeling that we should get rid of British imperialism, be free and make our own decisions," he remembers. "The idea was that our country should belong to us and we should be running the country. We were revolutionaries at a young age."

The general unrest continued to build. The Bhatia family heard every week about new protests, riots, and popular movements designed to change the existing order. Gurcharan was part of this movement, and he did his part by hiding rebel leaders in his family home in Jammu. The political situation in India had escalated as the Second World War dragged to an end in 1945. Indian leaders called for freedom, and many of the colonial authorities and police were on high alert, searching for rebel leaders. They kept a close watch on the activities of these men, and tracked their travels.

At the time, Gurcharan's family had a relatively large house with a spacious living room. When freedom fighting rebel leaders escaped from other regions of India into Jammu and Kashmir, Gurcharan and the other student leaders decided to hide these wanted men in the home of the police superintendent, thinking it was the last place authorities would look. Gurcharan brought the rebel leaders to his parents' home in Jammu. Gurcharan's mother was a hospitable woman who never guessed the identity of her guests. She offered food and shelter to the guests, without realizing they were freedom fighters. Gurcharan's siblings were too young to guess what was happening, and his father was away on duty in Mirpur.

Gurcharan, and his friends Ved Bhasin and Balraj Puri, knew it was important to keep their activities secret. They did not allow many people to visit the strangers so that local police never knew what was happening. Even though Gurcharan was acting without his father's consent, he still respected him. He guessed the elder Bhatia knew what he was doing. Perhaps some of Ishar's co-workers were aware of his son's activities, too and Ishar certainly knew about his son's interest in the freedom movement. In one instance, Gurcharan's father confronted his son about the matter.

"My job is on the line," Ishar told him. "If you are doing something illegal, you need to tell me."

Gurcharan replied: "I am interested in the freedom movement and I will try to help in whatever way possible. If you want to take me to jail, you can. But at the same time, you have to charge me for something and there's no evidence yet."

Gurcharan's father told him his actions might have consequences for his own position, and he warned his son not to do anything that would cause problems for the family. He never explicitly told his son to stop sheltering freedom fighters. Out of respect for his father and his father's job, Gurcharan tried to keep a low profile in the movement. Gurcharan never made public statements or speeches at student rallies or marches, although his friend Balraj and Ved did. The three friends met with many others every day to make plans to help the independence movement. Amid the social and political unrest, activists organized meetings for communities and men and women. Student leaders like Ved and Balraj took the initiative to try and reduce the growing tensions among various religious groups. Sadly, the students recognized communal violence could become a reality. Gurcharan never felt he was a leader, even though he was heavily involved in these activities. Working on these campaigns with other students engaged and excited him more than anything else. Like the rest of the country, he waited with anticipation for August 15, 1947, the night India would achieve independence.

———— ∞ ————

Gurcharan's mother wanted him to celebrate his birthday with family and friends, but he was off with his friends in the student movement, roaming the city. His western birthday is August 2, 1931, but the Indian calendar has rotational dates, so Gurcharan's birthday fell on August 15th in 1947. Gurcharan's mother baked him a cake, but he was too busy to stay home for a party. Instead, Gurcharan, Ved and other students invited local leaders who supported secularism and human rights to lead peace committees in all areas of the city. These leaders represented different religions and ethnic backgrounds. Riots had erupted in other areas of India, and the student leaders wanted to extinguish any possibility of communal violence in their own hometown, so they brought people together to talk about peace. That day, Gurcharan and other student leaders held a public meeting in the parade grounds to encourage people to keep peace, look after their neighbours and avoid all conflict.

"Basically our whole family was wondering what would happen," Gurcharan remembered. "We sometimes felt that we had reached the end of the rainbow with a golden pot—but that pot was not full of gold, but full of problems, particularly related to communal strife and killings."

The family was particularly worried about the threat of violence in the newly created nation of Pakistan. Gurcharan's mother feared for her two sisters, her parents and other relatives, some of whom were living in Gujranwala, a city which would become part of the new Muslim country. Other relatives lived near Sialkot, which was also destined to become part of Pakistan. Gurcharan's father was stationed near the border to keep the peace. He was on 24-hour active duty in charge of the security forces in Mirpur.

Radios were still uncommon, so the Bhatia family and others gathered around the radio at another family's house to listen to the speeches of Prime Minister Nehru. They were excited because the British were leaving India after three hundred years of rule. This brought hope, but people were still nervous about what would happen after the partition of the old British colonial territory into the two independent nations of India and Pakistan.

Viceroy Lord Mountbatten presented the plan for partition on June 3, 1947. The plan shaped India and Pakistan into two separate countries. Gandhi and Nehru opposed the idea, but they did not win the argument due to the insistence of the Muslim League for a separate Muslim nation. Indians learned they would be able to govern themselves by June 1948.

As Britain retreated, India and Pakistan exploded. Hindus in Pakistan were victims of riots and communal violence, while Muslims in India were also suffering from riots that erupted at many places in India. Hindus from Pakistan scrambled to the Punjab, hoping for safety in the region that overlapped the two nations. People wanted to live in the nation to which they felt a connection and loyalty; they didn't want to choose their home for religious reasons alone. Some people moved to join family members living on the other side. Others wondered how resources and businesses could be divided fairly and if Muslim business owners living in India would have to cross the border to live and work in Pakistan. The new line on the maps divided thousands of people from family members and relatives.

During the turmoil of partition, more than twelve million people were displaced and hundreds of thousands died violently. Most of the movement between the two countries occurred in Bengal and Punjab, which had a direct impact on the Bhatia family and their relatives. The partition of India is remembered for its massacres, bloodshed and extreme, horrific acts of violence. Muslims, Sikhs and Hindus were perpetrators as well as victims of violence involving knives, swords, guns, torture and rape. No one was safe. Children, the elderly and the sick were murdered along with everyone else. Looting and robbery became common. The perpetrators' aim was not only to kill people, but to torture people, break them, and destroy their will to live. Riots throughout the country resulted in millions of refugees, economic disruption and social unrest.

Living next to the Punjab, the Bhatia family found itself near one of the areas that experienced the most violence. Mirpur was on the border of the newly created Pakistan, and Jammu was not far away. Immediately after independence, independent Pakistani raiders entered the disputed territory of Kashmir and began killing innocent Hindus and Sikhs so they could try to take over the administration of the government. Kashmiri ruler Maharajah Hari Singh and Sheikh Abdullah asked the government of India to intervene. The Indian leadership sent its army to fight against the invading Pakistanis who had recruited Afghans and others to their cause. War broke out in Kashmir. The United Nations eventually became involved, but the dispute was not resolved and it endures today.

Throughout the chaos, Ishar continued to work in Mirpur. A popular Sikh leader named Baba Mohan controlled a gurdwara that offered food to Hindus, Sikhs and Muslims in the area. Two months before the massacres started, Ishar advised Baba to leave the dangerous area and move to Kampur in Uttar Pradesh, two hundred kilometres from Delhi.

"This shows my father had the inkling that bad things were going to happen, but he never told us," recalled Gurcharan. "Sometimes we would say we wanted to go and stay with him in Mirpur, but he kept telling us to stay where we were and he would come and meet us. He had some kind of feeling that there would be disaster in the area. I think he anticipated that things would not be good."

Ishar's strong sense of duty contributed to his fate. When massacres began in the region, and angry hordes of Hindus and Muslims began fighting, Ishar worked to move refugees out of the area, trying to save as many people as possible.

"He could have been one of the first people to go," said Gurcharan. "There were other police and government employees who escaped and came back to Jammu before everyone else."

Vigilante intruders from Pakistan were civilians spurred by the unrest, and they attacked and invaded the border area near Mirpur. Few people had access to radio, telephone or television, so they had to rely on word of mouth to hear the news. All non-Muslims were asked to assemble at safe houses throughout the city, including the gurdwara. They were ordered to flee immediately before the armed invaders approached.

Local government had collapsed and people had no police or military to restore order. Families had little food and no access to milk. Gurcharan's grandparents and other Mirpur residents could hardly believe what they were hearing. To save their own lives, they abandoned their ancestral land and homes, leaving their possessions behind. No one had ever had to evacuate Mirpur before, not even when raiders from the north and Middle East had invaded. Now hundreds of people left in groups of fifty and began walking or riding their donkeys towards Jammu. They lacked food, water and emergency supplies.

Gurcharan's grandparents, by now in their nineties, left with a small group and walked through mountains filled with Muslim antagonists. As they trudged the hot, dirt road to freedom, the mob stalked them. The Pakistanis carried large swords and guns, and they caught up to the walkers and attacked them. They preferred to attack the young and able bodied, and sexually assaulted young women and girls before stabbing them. Older people were left untouched because they were considered less of a threat. The refugees could not escape the violence; they found no restaurants, hotels or shelters along the way for refuge. Pakistani raiders apprehended some walkers and hacked them to death with swords and knives while other refugees were shot. Girls and women were picked off and abducted. Some walkers who escaped the violence succumbed to the elements and died of exhaustion or starvation along the way.

Gurcharan, his mother and his siblings, learned that his aunts had been abducted from Mirpur and likely tortured or raped and killed. Mirpur was a small city, and everyone living there knew the Bhatia family. Upon arriving in Jammu, refugees shared their tragic stories. The people of Jammu knew people were still fleeing from Mirpur and they wanted to help them. India had no Red Cross or other social security agencies at the time, so volunteers boarded buses and went to meet refugees in the desert. Gurcharan was eager to help the refugees and joined the cause.

One group of volunteers found Gurcharan's grandparents, who had only managed to travel about eighty kilometres from Mirpur in a week due to their advanced age and the difficult terrain. Gurcharan took the bus to the halfway point to meet them, helping other refugees along the way. The long, harrowing walk had exhausted his grandparents. They were devastated and traumatized by the ordeal.

Sixty-seven family members, including many of their own children, were dead or missing.

Kulwant was unable to join the volunteers because she had to stay home and take care of her children. She was growing increasingly worried about Ishar. At first, refugees told the Bhatia family he was still in Mirpur, trying to help Hindus and Sikhs leave the city. She knew the violence was escalating. In the days that followed, the chaos continued. Muslims were killing Sikhs and Hindus in an attempt to capture the largest possible area to add to Pakistan.

"It was complete lawlessness," recalled Gurcharan. "People had machetes, swords and guns and they were using any weapon to kill and there was no one to check them." His mother was a spiritual woman and she turned to prayer. Eventually her fears for her husband became reality. People arriving from Mirpur had no more news about Ishar.

The Bhatia family never learned what happened to Ishar Singh Bhatia. He did not call home or send a message, and none of the refugees arriving from Mirpur had any news about his activities or whereabouts. The Bhatia family became frantic and tried to contact anyone who might be able to tell them whether Ishar was dead or alive. Kulwant was unable to cope, prayed constantly, and followed any advice given to her. "People would tell her to pray, and religious seers would try to tell her where her husband was," said Gurcharan. "She would believe every word because she wanted to know what had happened and where he was."

Even on her deathbed, Kulwant never accepted Ishar's death and offered suggestions on where people should look for her husband, even though no one had seen him for decades. She believed he had escaped and was imprisoned in another country. She tried to go to Pakistan to find her husband, but the Indian government declared it too dangerous and forbid her from entering the country. Kulwant persisted and kept visiting police officers and government officials, who couldn't do anything to help her. She couldn't accept that Ishar was dead, because no one had witnessed the killing. It took years for the Bhatia family to give up the hope that he was alive.

Ishar's disappearance meant the family no longer had any income. They were also unable to collect life insurance from the government, as they had no way of proving that Ishar was dead. Gurcharan, who was sixteen when he became the patriarch of his family, believes his father died trying to save others. He couldn't have escaped the invading Pakistani raiders due to the geography and isolation of Mirpur.

Civil unrest spread to Jammu. Bombings and large riots rocked India's cities, and Muslims and non-Muslims continued to fight and kill each other. Food was becoming increasingly expensive. Gurcharan consoled and assisted his mother, accompanying her to various places to search for his father. He arranged meetings with people who knew his father and attempted to learn more about the fate of his relatives.

At times Gurcharan wondered if he should pick up a sword or gun and fight along with the others. His mother was quick to dissuade him and told him violence would never help the situation. Kulwant followed Gandhi's instructions, and reminded Gurcharan that peace was always the better option. Gurcharan collected baby formula and food for refugees. Helping others made him feel better. "It was a really bad situation," he recalled. "People said to us, 'Muslims have killed your father and your relatives, and you are trying to save them.' It was an emotionally charged atmosphere. People had absolutely no rational thinking."

The Bhatia family focused on surviving the chaos around them. Trucks filled the streets of Jammu. The Indian army used the road in front of the Bhatia home to travel from Jammu to the summer capital of Srinagar in Kashmir. Thousands of Indian army personnel travelled through Jammu to fight the invaders from Pakistan. Refugees from neighbouring areas filled the streets, searching for shelter. Gurcharan and his family and friends gave shelter to refugees they knew, but couldn't help the others. People tried to contact government, social workers and other forms of assistance, but there was no aid available. Schools closed and the city was under curfew.

"You couldn't even get out of the house sometimes," said Gurcharan. "We didn't know what to do. We were living from minute to minute, hour to hour."

The Bhatia family needed to escape Jammu. Kulwant was becoming increasingly worried because their savings were dwindling. The family was not penniless, but they had no income. Gurcharan's uncle intervened, and the family soon found themselves leaving the chaos of Jammu for the safer haven of New Delhi.

CHAPTER 4

A YOUNG REFUGEE

Avtar Singh, Gurcharan's uncle, was concerned about his family members in Jammu. He wrote to his sister and told her to bring her family to New Delhi where they could apply to be refugees, stay safe and receive assistance from the federal government. New Delhi was the capital of the new India, so family members could encourage the Indian embassy to search for Ishar and other missing family members. At first, the Bhatias hesitated. How could they flee Jammu when they were so worried about other family members in the region? Finally, Gurcharan's grandfather urged them to leave.

"I have lost all of my children, my brother and my sister and everything," the older man told the family. "Now you people have to get educated and need to work. You need to go to Delhi."

The widow travelled by train to her brother's home Delhi with her four children. Her first priority was to enrol them in school. Avtar Singh opened his home to Gurcharan's family, to another sister and her family, and to his parents. Avtar could not accommodate all of the relatives for long, and the Bhatias moved to a refugee home as soon as one became available. The house at 10 Lady Harding Road had previously belonged to a Muslim family who had fled after the partition. Many Muslim homes in the area were abandoned, and the Minister of Refugees seized the homes and gave them to refugees.

Gurcharan has strong memories of the house at Lady Harding Road, shared with his immediate family, and two of Kulwant's sisters and their families. The house had four or five bedrooms, and all five members of the Bhatia family lived in one bedroom. His mother's younger sister and her family occupied another bedroom, while a man named Bahadar Singh and his family occupied a third bedroom. More than twenty people occupied the home, so they cooked on an open cooking system in the driveway because there was only one kitchen inside.

Life began to resume some degree of normalcy. Gurcharan and his siblings returned to school. Gurcharan was able to walk to the government refugee camp college, located in tents a few blocks away from their home. While living at his uncle's house, he had had to take the bus across town to go to school. The city of New Delhi was largely peaceful, but it was buckling under the weight of its refugees, and the city's infrastructure suffered. Prior to partition, only a million people lived in Delhi. The newly arrived refugees needed housing, schools and transportation. Gurcharan felt the effects of the crowding when he tried to board the bus. There were times when the bus was full, and he would have to walk the long distance to school.

Gurcharan remembers grieving his family's loss, but he knew he was not the only one grieving. Many people living in the refugee home were dealing with their tragedies. Gurcharan found it useful to share his grief with others and realized that other people had problems bigger than his own. He helped his mother, finished his high school courses and enrolled in early university courses. "Life was busy, but simple," he remembers.

The Bhatias flourished in their new location. Gurcharan's youngest sister, Surinder, took a job with the government. His other sister, Kuldip, was accepted at nursing college on scholarship due to her high grades. By 1950, she was enrolled at nursing college and studying in the evenings. Manjit was eight years younger than Gurcharan, so he was still in primary school. Kulwant continued her search for Ishar, consulting with religious seers and fortune-tellers to try to determine what had happened to her husband. She frequently went to the gurdwara to pray.

Gurcharan was feeling better about life, and he was still determined to make money for his family. He wanted to find a job, but his mother wanted him to pursue an education so he would be able to seek better employment. Avtar was a chartered accountant in Delhi, and he asked Gurcharan to study accounting as well and offered to pay him to study. This was almost unheard of at the time since students who articled in accounting firms had to pay for their own apprenticeships. Accounting, engineering and medicine were considered the three best career options for young Indians.

Yet Gurcharan felt conflicted. He had a strong sense of duty and believed he wasn't living up to the promise he'd made to his father to take care of the family. "Life was still very confusing," he said. "I was always feeling that we were set up and living in a house, but someone had to make money." Gurcharan decided that it was more important to earn money right away, so he ran off to Bombay to work.

Many young people rebel by smoking, drinking or breaking curfew. Gurcharan decided to rebel by finding a job at a local railway in Bombay. He was inspired to head to Bombay when he saw an advertisement looking for people to work in the train offices. He didn't want his family members to convince him not to go, so he left without telling them.

Gurcharan found work as a ticket collector for Bombay's local light rail transit. He moved into the local gurdwara and took his meals there as well. Refugees from Pakistan and other parts of India filled the gurdwara, so it was a difficult place to live. On his first day on the job, Gurcharan discovered corruption. He was to take money from fishermen who were transferring from countryside cars to Bombay's local rail system. In the early mornings, the fishermen carried large baskets of fish with them as they travelled to local markets. To Gurcharan's surprise, the fishermen didn't give Gurcharan tickets. Instead, they put money directly into his pockets. Gurcharan didn't understand what was happening. At noon, Gurcharan went to his supervisor and gave him all the money from the morning. The supervisor told him the money belonged to Gurcharan and all the other railway workers.

"You mean we are taking bribes?" he asked. "They are not buying tickets?"

His supervisor replied, "You give the money to me and I will pass it on."

Gurcharan did not want to be involved in corrupt practices, but knew it was important to keep the job. He told his supervisor he would not take the bribes and he returned the money. Yet he still needed a way to escape from the situation. So he lied to his supervisor and told him he was allergic to the smell of fish. The smell was going to make him sick, and he needed to be transferred to another part of the station. He told his supervisor that he knew the general manager of the railway and would tell about the corrupt practices. The supervisor was upset, but transferred him.

Even though it had been his choice to run away, Gurcharan still felt uncertain about his actions. He wrote to his mother and told her where he was. At the same time, his mother and uncle had started hunting for him by contacting relatives. A distant family member owned a hotel in Bombay, and Avtar and Kulwant convinced relatives to go to the gurdwara to visit Gurcharan. They ordered him to quit his job and return to New Delhi, telling him that his mother was upset by his disappearance. They reminded him she had already lost Ishar, and his decision to go to Bombay only escalated her grief. His relatives' appeal moved Gurcharan and he returned home after a month. He never collected his salary in person. Instead, the money was mailed to his home in Delhi.

"I think there are two sides to every picture," recalled Gurcharan. "When I went to Bombay, I think I became a man. I went from a little boy to a man. I started thinking a lot and looking at people in the refugee camps. I went to refugee camps and met children who had no home, no food—children who had lost relatives in Pakistan. I saw how they were managing life. The governments couldn't do much. The refugees were drinking dirty water, eating whatever they could get. The local communities were getting together to help them. It was the lower rungs of the population who were bringing volunteers to help. The people who were poor were helping more. This was eye opening for me. Life is a question of survival."

When he returned to his home, Gurcharan, Avtar and Kulwant discussed the issue. Kulwant told him she understood his desire to earn money for the family, but she wanted education to be his priority. She suggested they find a way for Gurcharan to work while going to school. Gurcharan went back to evening college, leaving his days free for work in his uncle's office. He passed his university exams but still needed to take courses, apprentice, study and pass more exams to become a chartered accountant. During this time, he won a scholarship for Kashmiri students, allowing him to attend one of the best engineering colleges in the country, the Indian Institute of Technology in Roorke, in Uttar Pradesh. Gurcharan attended the college for a week, decided it was not for him, and returned the scholarship.

Instead, he worked with his uncle for four years and continued to help others in the student movement to advocate for refugee students. Many refugee students had no residences while they were studying, and they were not eligible for scholarships or loans. Gurcharan and his friends asked the government for funds, professors and resources for the camp colleges. As a member of the Kashmiri students' association in New Delhi, he also advocated for democratic reforms in his home state. The students supported secular rule in India and believed all religions were equal and could co-exist. Gurcharan and his friends wanted a democratic regime with an elected national assembly for Kashmir.

By this time, Sheikh Abdullah, a Muslim who supported Gandhi's ideals and supported secularism in India, was prime minister of Jammu and Kashmir and was the state's most important political figure. The Pakistani government viewed Sheikh Abdullah as one of Nehru's agents and refused to recognize his leadership.

Balraj Puri and Ved Bhasin were also in Delhi, and they welcomed Sheikh Abdullah and other Kashmiri leaders as visitors to the college. Gurcharan and his friends organized receptions for Sheikh Abdullah and the other leaders, who spoke to the students about communal harmony. During this period, Gurcharan and his friends held Sheikh Abdullah in high esteem because he was supporting the Indian National Congress and opposed the Maharajah of Kashmir.

Balraj Puri has remained a lifelong friend. "He was my mentor in many ways," recalled Gurcharan. "He was always interested in Jammu and Kashmir and wanted them together as an integral unit. He promot-ed communal harmony among Hindus, Muslims, Sikhs and Buddhists. Balraj was very popular with various groups and was knowledgeable about communities and their leaders. He used the media to discuss problems."

Balraj, who is three years older than Gurcharan, became a journalist. He started his first newspaper when he was thirteen years old, and even-tually wrote several highly acclaimed books about Jammu and Kashmir and the political struggle in the region. He is also known for his work as a human rights activist and Indian political commentator.

Over time, Gurcharan and his friends noticed that some of the Kashmiri leaders in government had become corrupt. The leaders were preaching Gandhian principles, but were not following them. Violence in Jammu and Kashmir continued with riots involving Hindus, Muslims and Sikhs. "We noticed these Kashmiri leaders had all the power and were becoming like dictators. There were no checks and balances, and they had an unlimited amount of money at their disposal," said Gurcharan. He and his friends arranged a meeting with the country's most famous politician to express their concerns.

CHAPTER 5

MEETING NEHRU

F ew people would think to request a meeting with their prime minister, but Gurcharan Singh Bhatia and Balraj Puri felt compelled to do what they believed was right. They feared that the government of Kashmir was becoming a dictatorship. They worried about the ongoing war-like conditions and government corruption in the region and wanted a democratic assembly with free elections.

"If you see there is a need for something, and you feel strongly about it, you should do something about it, not just talk about it. Do something rather than talk about things," said Gurcharan, explaining his decision to request a meeting with Prime Minister Jawaharlal Nehru.

The two friends wrote to Nehru's office on behalf of the Kashmiri students' union in Delhi. Nehru, who was Kashmiri, likely had a special concern about the region, too. His secretary wrote back to Gurcharan and Balraj, and told them the prime minister was willing to meet with them. Avtar was sitting in his office when a bike courier pedalled up to deliver a letter for Gurcharan, who had sent the request from his uncle's office. Surprised, Avtar wondered why his nephew was receiving a letter from the prime minister. Balraj and Gurcharan were thrilled with the response. Kulwant and Avtar were excited about the meeting, too, even though they wondered what two students would have to say to the prime minister. Gurcharan and Balraj wrote out their presentation with care, explaining their desire for an elected assembly in Jammu and Kashmir. Their first meeting with Nehru lasted about an hour. Gurcharan remembers Nehru as gracious and interested in what they had to say. The prime minister was passionate and used his hand to thump on the table while they were discussing democracy; he said that Kashmir would never go to Pakistan. "Nehru said, 'Democracy or no democracy, Kashmir will stay in India. We are there with power, not with democracy, and we will stay there.'"

Gurcharan and Balraj told Nehru that everyone in India would lose if democracy were not restored to Kashmir. Nehru listened to their opinions and suggested the students meet with Minister Gopalaswami Iyengar, the minister in charge of Kashmiri affairs. Iyengar agreed with the students, but made no promises. However, Gurcharan and Balraj hoped that there would be changes in the region. After three years of watching the Kashmiri crisis, Balraj and Gurcharan wrote to Nehru again. In their letter, they said, "We followed your advice and met with the Kashmiri ministers. We think the population of Kashmir is very unhappy with the dictatorship and the police state. If we have democracy, the people will be able to vent their feelings and we will have representatives for the people. The people will not necessarily be pro-Pakistan."

By 1953 Sheikh Abdullah had started advocating for an independent Kashmir. The United States encouraged this proposal, believing an alliance with a free Kashmir would give Americans better access to the surrounding nations. Sheikh Abdullah began holding meetings with the communists in his government. The government of India feared that Sheikh Abdullah would make statements against India, because the international community, including the United Nations, had placed India on a human rights watch due to the continuing violence.

During their second meeting with Nehru, Gurcharan and Balraj urged the prime minister to restore democracy in Kashmir so that the people living in the area would continue to support India. They were concerned about the ongoing violence and the lack of political freedom. They thought the Indian government seemed afraid of Sheikh Abdullah. Gurcharan and Balraj found Nehru had changed and was not as idealistic about the problems in Kashmir as he had been in the past.

"Nehru had such a huge role in the freedom movement of India," said Gurcharan. "He was always talking about democracy, human rights and equality. When we met him the second time, that image was jarred because he had become a practical politician."

Nehru told the students he planned to keep the army in Kashmir whether or not democracy was restored. Balraj and Gurcharan were disappointed and told Nehru that Kashmir, India and the international community would lose faith in the new nation. Nehru said he wanted the students to keep him up to date on the events in Kashmir and he wanted to create an elected assembly in Kashmir. The two friends met with other ministers who were handling the Kashmir issue. Finally, those in power acted. Sheikh Abdullah was jailed August 8, 1953 and imprisoned for eleven years.

The Bhatia family was still living in the refugee house and wished to own a home. They were finally able to collect Ishar's life insurance and buy a small house in New Delhi, thanks to a program of the Oriental Insurance Company, which allotted insurance payments to families that hadn't heard from relatives for more than five years. It pained the Bhatia family to admit that Ishar was dead. Their new home, built by the Indian government, was a two-room house located on a small lot in Nizamuddin East. The Bhatia family had to wait for a home for longer than they wished because they had a difficult time acquiring refugee status. The government still could not determine if Jammu and Kashmir belonged to India or Pakistan.

The house was in a beautiful location, across the street from a famous monument known as Humayun's Tomb. Built prior to the creation of the Taj Mahal, the tomb likely influenced the design of the more famous monument. Gurcharan took his books to the site and studied in the park around the tomb or within the tomb itself if it happened to be raining. Each morning, Kulwant would give him breakfast and send him out to study so he wouldn't be disturbed. She even brought his lunch to the tomb so he wouldn't return home and be tempted to socialize with friends who were constantly stopping by the house. Gurcharan spent his time studying and earned extra money with accounting work for three different businesses. He was happy to be helping his family financially at last. "For ten years, I didn't see a movie or go to a restaurant. We were always busy, either working or helping refugees or working with the student movement," he said.

In 1955 Gurcharan passed his examination to become a chartered accountant. He returned to work in the accounting business with his uncle. His new dream was to go overseas to earn a degree in business at the Royal College of Science and Technology in Glasgow. Gurcharan had learned about the college from members of the Scottish business elite in New Delhi. He worked hard for two years, saving his money so he could study business management and administration. At last the young Indian was ready to leave his country for the first time. He set off to seek adventure and knowledge.

CHAPTER 6

GLASGOW LESSONS

Gurcharan's journey to Britain began with a two-week ocean voyage. He travelled from Bombay to Southampton, England, through the Suez Canal. Four friends from India travelled with him and he managed to make new friends on the boat, too.

Gurcharan has always made friends easily, partly because he loves talking to people and asking them questions about their lives. His natural curiosity engages others, and his ability to listen creates connections. "You have to have interest in other people and let them feel comfortable. That's very important," he said. "My friends are my biggest asset. They have always been very helpful. Living in India during the partition made people feel they had to stick together, stay close and work together."

Before Gurcharan left for his trip, Avtar told his nephew to tip the waiters on the ship during his first day on board. The waiters responded to Gurcharan's charity, and he enjoyed cookies and sweets for the entire journey. In London, Gurcharan and his friends sought out the cheapest and best food, and later ate dinner at the Indian consulate. The staff members were friendly and offered to assist the young Indians as they were in a new land and had few social contacts or friends.

Gurcharan took the train from London to Glasgow. One of his uncle's friends lived in Glasgow and he took Gurcharan to the college.

Most students rented places throughout the city, but Gurcharan set up residence in a hostel, affiliated with Chesters College in Bearsden, located about ten miles from Glasgow. His living quarters were inexpensive, only seven pounds a week for room and board. Arriving on a weekend, Gurcharan set off for a coffee shop. A Scotsman approached him, telling him he'd been to India and had lots of friends in the Punjab. The Scotsman was already drunk, and wanted to welcome Gurcharan to Scotland. He ordered two scotches, one for himself and one for the newcomer. When Gurcharan told him he didn't drink alcohol, the Scotsman drank both drinks himself, toasting the student with each glass. He continued to order more drinks, raising his glass each time, while telling stories about Scotland. He offered to introduce the foreign student to his new city. Gurcharan was touched by the drunken man's hospitality, but declined the offer.

Even though Gurcharan looked different from the Scottish people, he found that they were quick to accept him. Since he is a Sikh, he wears a turban and beard, and refrains from cutting his hair. He wears a small steel bracelet, known as the *kara,* around his wrist. The kara is worn on the right wrist, symbolizing that the wearer is married to truth. Many Scots had been to India, or had relatives who had been to India because of British involvement in the subcontinent. Gurcharan had never experienced the western world before, but most Scottish people were familiar with Indian culture. He also located a Sikh gurdwara in Glasgow.

On Monday morning, Gurcharan hurried to campus. It was still dark when he entered his classroom, and he was two minutes late. Christopher MacRae, principal of the school, stood in front of the class, delivering a lecture to the entire student body. MacRae had a PhD in philosophy and taught in the management college. When Gurcharan entered the room, MacRae addressed him in front of everyone else. "Mr. Bhatia, here we work not with the sun, but with the clock."

The statement was an acknowledgement of Gurcharan's tardiness and a reference to his Indian heritage. MacRae was implying that Indians had a more fluid concept of punctuality and that Gurcharan needed to abide by the western concept of time. Only two other South Asian students attended the college with Gurcharan: a Muslim student from Pakistan and a Hindu student from Uttar Pradesh. Gurcharan was inspired and impressed by MacRae's lecture, and one of the professor's ideas stayed with him for the rest of his life. "The shortest distance between two points is a straight line," said MacRae. "You must have a clear focus of your destination. If you don't have a clear focus, you can go right or left, but that will prolong your journey. You must know what direction you are heading."

Gurcharan interpreted this statement as advice to study harder and accomplish his goals. He had cultivated a habit of going to bed and rising early. Many of his classmates would study until 2 a.m., but Gurcharan went to bed at 10 p.m. and rose at 4 a.m. On weekends, he didn't go out with the others, but stayed inside reading or studying in the library. He knew he had to finish all of his courses within two years or he would exhaust his savings. During the summer holidays, the college found him a work project in the James Buchanan Scotch distillery. Gurcharan's task was to devise a system to make better use of the wood used to construct the wooden casks. After two months at the distillery, he wrote a report about his strategy and received £1,000 for his efforts. He submitted his paper to the college and received full marks.

Many students at the college were curious about Gurcharan's turban. He encouraged their questions, as he felt it was his duty to teach others about his culture and spiritual background. He believed that educating people about Sikhs and their religious beliefs was the best way to break down stereotypes and introduce himself to people.

Gurcharan achieved his goal of completing all of his courses in two years. He was awarded the Turnbull Prize for top marks. He bought a used car for £40 and spent a month travelling around Europe with four other students. One of these students was Sukhbir Singh Dhupia, who became a lifelong friend. Dhupia returned to India, joined Imperial Chemical Industries and became a director of the company.

While in London, Gurcharan had an eye-opening experience. "There were about twenty-five visitors in a museum," he recalled. "The guide asked what country they had come from, and all of them said they were from Canada." Gurcharan was surprised because the group was so ethnically diverse and included Caucasians, African Canadians, Asian Canadians and even a few Sikhs.

"I said, 'My God, Canada!' I had thought all Canadians were white, and these people were a mixture. I talked to some people and they were impressed with their country and were talking about Canada being their home and how happy they were in Canada." The experience affected Gurcharan and he wondered how people from so many different nations could find peace in the same country. "Subconsciously, I was developing an attraction for Canada."

After his travels around Europe, Gurcharan took the ship back to Bombay. When he arrived in India, he saw his culture with an outsider's eyes. During his two years away from his country, he had often dreamed about his return to his homeland. His biggest desire was to chew a betel leaf. But when he saw a customs official chewing a betel leaf, he found that he was disgusted by the man's stained red teeth and the ugly colouring around his mouth. As Gurcharan watched, the man spat a wad against a wall. Gurcharan was completely repulsed and has never again eaten a betel leaf.

He returned to his family home in New Delhi and started to work in his uncle's new business. Avtar had purchased a travel agency, Iyer and Sons Limited in Connaught Circus, New Delhi, hoping to attract Indians who had just started to travel abroad. Gurcharan's first day as general manager was not without its challenges. When he reported to work, he found the door locked and the staff on strike. He called the staff leader to arrange a meeting to learn about the situation. Gurcharan and two staff members had an extended dinner, which began at 4 p.m. and ended long after midnight.

Fortunately, Gurcharan had studied the art of negotiation and was determined to cooperate with staff, end the strike and create a better work environment. He told the staff members: "As long as the doors are locked, neither staff nor management is making any money. Clients will disappear, which is dangerous for the business. We need to make a decision quickly and have a deadline for the resolution of problems. If we don't solve the problems by the deadline, the staff can strike again. We can't damage this business."

Gurcharan and the staff members were able to reach an agreement. The staff had been striking over pay and holiday time, and Gurcharan met their demands. One of the managers, Akleshram Iyer, a Hindu from the south, did not want to come to work before 11 a.m. because he wanted to pray before work. He won permission as long as he stayed later to make up his hours. Under Gurcharan's management, the business flourished. Focusing his attention on his career, he wasn't thinking about romance. His marriage came as a surprise to him.

CHAPTER 7

JITI

In 1962, Gurcharan married a beautiful, intelligent woman he had never spoken to. She would become the love of his life and his soul mate.

The relationship began with an innocent trip to the mountains. Gurcharan had met his friend, Shiv Kholsa, in primary school. While Gurcharan was studying abroad, Shiv had become a major in the army with a new post at Simla, a five-hour drive away from Delhi. Shiv invited Gurcharan to visit him in the mountains, see the snow and meet Bubbal, his new wife. As the three young Indians sat and watched the snow fall, Bubbal asked Gurcharan, now in his early thirties, why he hadn't married. Gurcharan told her he hadn't met the right woman. Bubbal asked him to describe his ideal.

Gurcharan said he wanted to marry a woman who could enjoy friendships with the many people in his life. He needed someone who was comfortable entertaining and engaging strangers, since his social life was a priority. He also wanted a true partner who could help him take care of his family, especially his aging mother.

As soon as Gurcharan finished talking, Bubbal said, "I know this girl."

"Where is she?" asked Gurcharan.

"She's in Calcutta," said Bubbal. "She's a good friend of mine and I know her very well. She's just the girl you are looking for."

Gurcharan was intrigued but didn't take the conversation seriously. Two days after he returned to Delhi from Simla, he received an envelope in the mail. He looked at the enclosed photograph of a young woman and realized Bubbal was serious about matchmaking. Gurcharan likes to joke that he was surrounded by matchmakers and had no way to escape from his marriage.

Jagjit Puri, known as Jiti, was born September 21, 1937 and was one of ten children. She was educated and had a bachelor's degree in history and geography. Like the Bhatias, the Puris had a strong belief in the importance of education for all family members. Her father was a well-established banker in Calcutta who knew many people in Delhi. Gurcharan was also popular because of his successful travel business. Partap Singh, manager of the Imperial Hotel in New Delhi, was good friends with Jiti's father and knew Gurcharan, too. He arranged a lunch date with Gurcharan and began praising Jiti, saying she was a good girl with many talents and virtues. Gurcharan had not spoken to any of his family members about getting married. He had been preoccupied with his sisters' marriages and his brother's education. But the plans were set in motion and Jiti's father contacted Avtar to talk about the potential marriage. Avtar was enthused and told Kulwant, who was overjoyed at the prospect. Jiti's uncle, Balbir Singh, owned the York restaurant in New Delhi. Balbir was good friends with Avtar, and he told the Bhatia family that Jiti and her family would be stopping in New Delhi on their way back from Mussoorie, where they had been on a summer vacation in the mountains. Gurcharan's mother and uncle were eager to meet Jiti and her family, and the Puris were eager to meet Gurcharan.

In India, marriage is about joining families together. About a dozen Bhatias and Puris met at the Gaylord restaurant. But Jiti and Gurcharan didn't have a chance to speak to one another. The families had tea and snacks, talked, and approved the romantic match. Two of Jiti's older brothers had already married, but she was the oldest girl in her family and the first to marry. In accordance with Sikh customs, the family exchanged sweets. Over the next couple of months, the families set the wedding date and planned.

Seven months after their engagement, the couple met at the altar. The wedding day was February 9, 1962, a date considered extremely unlucky according to Indian religious calendars. Since it was such an inauspicious day, no one else was getting married, and there had not been a wedding for months. Traditional Indian weddings are huge affairs with many guests. In many cases, people are often invited to several weddings on the same day. But since no one had been to a wedding for months and there were no other weddings in the city, Jiti and Gurcharan had almost full attendance at their wedding. The unlucky date had no effect on their marriage. Gurcharan refers to his wife as a "true joy." The couple has been married for more than fifty years.

Normally the groom travels to the bride's hometown for the wedding, but the Bhatias and Puris decided to hold the wedding in New Delhi. As part of his responsibilities, Gurcharan found a place for Jiti's family members to stay during the week of the wedding ceremony. Gurcharan's father's cousin, Manmohan Singh, was chief engineer with Public Works in India, and had access to a government bungalow on a two-acre lot in a prime location. It was the perfect accommodation for the Puris.

Gurcharan was happy and excited on his wedding day and wasn't nervous at all. Instead, he was thrilled to find a partner to share his life with him. He knew he was marrying into a good, close-knit, loving family whose values were similar to his own. He also thought his new wife was pretty, inside and out.

"I thought it was a good match," said Gurcharan. "It was not exactly the 6-49. I had met her friends and the people who had introduced her to us, and they talked highly of her as a good, family-oriented person. She was said to be a person who could love and share."

Gurcharan admires his wife and wishes he had some of her qualities. "She is far better than myself, because I was busy building up a career, education, and business and was always thinking about the future. It was her patience, attitude and capacity to handle the problems in the family that helped us. She had total responsibility and took care of the family, particularly when we moved to Canada. She even took care of me."

Sikh weddings involve a week of celebration. Before the wedding ceremony, the families hold a party known as a *sangeet*; family members gather to sing songs, play music, dance and celebrate. The wife of Jiti's eldest brother, Sunena, was a particularly good singer and led the songs. Jiti's brothers took turns playing the *tabla,* a small Indian drum.

Kulwant, Gurcharan's sisters and other relatives put large garlands of flowers around his neck. Avtar took on the role of the groom's father for the event. Gurcharan mounted a horse and paraded through the streets, accompanied by his wedding party of family members and friends. The group travelled to the bungalow to meet Jiti and her attendants for the formal part of the ceremony. Jiti's wedding party included Inderjit, the woman who had introduced Jiti to Bubbal. After the conversation in the mountains, Bubbal had contacted Inderjit, who involved her father to start the matchmaking process. Inderjit's father was a good friend of Jiti's father.

Jiti wore the garlands of flowers typically worn by Sikh brides. She had stars drawn on her forehead and wore heavy, elaborate necklaces. About twelve hundred guests attended the festivities and dined on food provided by the York restaurant. The couple was married on the lawn in front of the bungalow. Their wedding ceremony included recitations from the *Guru Granth Sahib,* the Sikh holy book. Jiti's father, Sunder Singh Puri, tied the couple together with a scarf and handed the end to Gurcharan, symbolizing Jiti's move from her father's house to her husband's. Both sides of the family gave gifts to the couple, and the bride and groom fed cake to each other. The newlyweds travelled to Rajasthan for their honeymoon.

Many North American friends are curious when they hear that Gurcharan and Jiti had an arranged marriage. Jiti said she never worried about marrying Gurcharan, and their situation was common in India, as most marriages were arranged. Jiti trusted her father as well as her friends and other relatives who had spent time and effort checking Gurcharan's references. She believes her marriage is successful because she and Gurcharan were brought up to believe that marriages are arranged and couples fall in love with each other after the wedding day. The Bhatias are dedicated to their partnership and are truly fond of each other. Jiti is Gurcharan's most trusted confidante and advisor, and they talk about everything. "Gurcharan always comes to me to talk because he knows I am there for him," she says. "I will tell him what I feel, but the decisions are always up to him."

Jiti noticed her husband's good qualities early in their marriage. She admires his ability to make friends and his willingness to help others. Their son Gurvinder said Jiti will often try and defend her husband's point of view, which strengthens their bond. The match was arranged by North American standards, he said, but the arrangements were not made blindly. "I don't think my mother's family would have picked some guy unless they were convinced he was the best thing for Mom. The families had strong ties and used good judgment so their marriage was on the right track from the beginning."

Gurcharan and Jiti have a long history of morning meetings. Jiti likes to sleep in, while Gurcharan wakes up at 5 or 6 a.m. to read newspapers or online news. Just before Jiti wakes, Gurcharan makes her tea and they sit down together and discuss their plans for the day. This ritual started in the early years of their marriage.

During their first few years together, Gurcharan worked at the travel agency and began to travel abroad to promote Indian tourism to Mexicans, Americans and Canadians. By the 1960s, tourism to India had increased. Gurcharan attended travel conventions and met travel agents in Los Angeles, Las Vegas and New York. Gurcharan and a group of Indian travel agents created a promotional travel brochure encouraging tourists to *"Visit India!"* The booklet was filled with pictures and facts about the country's top tourist destinations.

Gurcharan's sister Kuldip and her husband Tejraj had moved to Winnipeg in the early 1960s. On one of his overseas trips, Gurcharan visited her, explored the city and began to feel a love for the country. While touring Winnipeg and Toronto, he met overseas Indians who had positive things to say about their new lives in Canada. He also met many Indians who had settled in the United States, and their experiences were not as rosy. The United States was embroiled in civil rights issues between blacks and whites, and this didn't make Gurcharan feel confident about relocating his young family. He thought Canada was a calmer, more tolerant nation and it had a greater appeal for him.

Gurcharan was in Canada at a conference when his daughter Priti was born on November 30, 1962. With a new child and a happy marriage, Gurcharan started to dream about moving overseas with his family.

Gurcharan had been thinking about emigration for a long time. He began to investigate the possibility when he visited a friend working at the Canadian consulate in New Delhi. He wanted to leave India because he was still haunted by his memories of war and violence. Even though his life in New Delhi was peaceful, he was constantly reminded of communal riots, the war in Kashmir, the loss of his childhood home and his experiences as a refugee. The baby formula shortage was the last straw. As he entered the Canadian consulate, his friend remarked that he didn't look happy.

"I want to get out of this place as soon as possible, because we can't feed our little girl formula, even though I am prepared to pay for it," Gurcharan replied.

He told his friend he wanted to move to Canada, and began the long application process. Kuldip and Tejraj offered advice and helped the Bhatias through the procedure. Once the Bhatias received approval for immigration, they went for medical testing and were free to leave. In 1964, the Indian government did not allow Indian nationals to carry more than the equivalent of seven Canadian dollars when they moved out of the country. Jiti and Gurcharan received permission from the Reserve Bank of India to travel with about five thousand rupees, the equivalent of $1,000 Canadian. The Bhatias informed Jiti's family about their decision to move one week before they left the country.

In the 1960s, flights had to stop frequently to refuel, so the journey to Canada was arduous. The first leg of their journey took the Bhatias to Beirut, where they stayed in a hotel. They had only planned to stay for one day, but the airline lost their luggage. They had stored some of their money in their suitcase, so they had to wait for a few days until their luggage was returned to them. From Beirut, the Bhatias flew to Zurich and then to London, England, where they stayed for a week with a family friend. They traded their rupees for British pounds and bought warm winter clothes. Their new coats did little to prepare them for the shock of Canada's cold weather.

Jiti and Gurcharan on their wedding day

Gurcharan and Jiti surrounded by family members and friends on
their wedding day. *Left to right*: Inderjit. Avtar Singh, Lakhbir,
Gurcharan, Shiv Kholsa, Jiti, unidentified, Bubbal Kholsa,
Harinder (Jiti's sister) and Sunder Singh Puri (Jiti's father).

Gurcharan wearing flowers and surrounded by family members.
Left to right: Meharban Singh Dhupia, Kuku Sodhbans, Bharat Kumar
Dilwali, Avtar Singh, (uncle) Gurcharan, Surinder Bhatia (sister),
Kuldip Bhatia, (sister), Gian Kour(aunt), Kulwant, (mother),
Kailash Dilwali, Mr Dhameja, Kulwant Singh (cousin).

Gurcharan on a horse as part of the wedding procession.
Gurcharan with Kaka (nephew), Kailash Dilwali, (friend)
and Avtar Singh. (uncle)

Gurcharan and family in a traditional family portrait taken at
the time of departure of cousin Kalwant Bhatia for Europe:
Sitting: Left to Right: Ishar Kour, (grandmother), Kulwant, (mother),
Gian Kour (aunt), Kalwant Singh (cousin), Hazur Singh (grandfather).
Standing Left to Right: Surinder (sister), unidentified, Balbir Singh (cousin),
Avtar Singh (uncle), Kuldip (sister), Gurcharan Singh, Lakhbir Singh (cousin).

Gurcharan and Kashmiri student leaders with the President of India.
Left to right- Three unidentified student leaders, Ram Nath Mengi,
Dr. Rajendra Prasad (President of India), Nilamber Dev Sharma,
Mulkh Raj Saraf (journalist), Gurcharan, unidentified.

WINNIPEG

The ultimate measure of a man is not where he stands in moments of comfort and convenience, but where he stands at times of challenge and controversy.

~ MARTIN LUTHER KING, JR.

CHAPTER 8

TELL ME WHAT A CANADIAN LOOKS LIKE

"Where have you decided to take me?" Jiti asked her husband as she left the airport and experienced Winnipeg's harsh winds for the first time. The thermometers in Winnipeg had dipped to new lows, as the city broke a record for cold temperatures on December 11, 1964, the day the Bhatias landed in their new country. Even though she'd never been to Canada, Jiti hadn't feared the move until the cold winds blew against her face. She had only packed one suitcase for her trip. At this point, the couple was not sure if their move to Canada would be permanent. If life didn't work out in Canada, they planned to return to India in a few years.

Gurcharan's sister Kuldip and her husband Tejraj met the Bhatias at the airport. The airport was small and unimpressive to the Bhatia family, accustomed to busy cities and grand buildings. The place was almost deserted because of the cold. The Bhatias quickly cleared customs and felt welcomed immediately, even though they were freezing. They were impressed with the custom staff's care and attention, and were happy to get off the plane. Jiti was the most exhausted and just wanted to go to sleep. The family had been travelling for more than a week and their luggage had been lost twice. Priti was excited. She loved the snow, and kept staring at it and laughing. The Bhatias stayed with Kuldip and Tejraj for a month before moving to a one-bedroom, furnished apartment that cost $100 a month.

Tejraj and Gurcharan were the only two Sikh men living in Winnipeg in 1964. Tejraj had studied abroad in England and had returned to India before finding a job in Winnipeg as a veterinarian for the federal government. The Bhatia family was determined to be successful in their new home, and they tackled this project with their usual determination and dedication. Gurcharan's first goal was to find a job.

⸺ ◦⧜◦ ⸺

The employer completed the job interview with a smile. He told the applicant he could be hired the next day as long as he made an effort to look like a Canadian and remove his turban and beard.

Gurcharan had a quick-witted reply: "You tell me what a Canadian looks like and I'll tell you how I'll conform," he said. He did not back down. "I told him the turban stays," he recalled. "And it has stayed until this day."

Gurcharan wasn't worried about turning down that job or even about finding a position in Canada. He knew he had valuable business experience and a solid education. He had started applying for positions with accounting firms in Canada while he was still in India and had received letters of interest. He knew his prospects for employment were good.

Gurcharan and his family moved to Canada when Indian immigration was still in its infancy. Between 1904 and 1908, five thousand immigrants from India settled in Canada, mainly in British Columbia. The Canadian government, worried about the influx of Indians, limited Indian immigration in the years that followed. Even though India was part of the British Empire, racist attitudes prevailed. Indians were seen as subordinate and less desirable than British and white European immigrants. Attitudes about non-white immigration started to change in the

1960s. Canada abandoned its racially-based selection criteria in 1962, in part because Prime Minister Lester B. Pearson found the racist policy abhorrent. Canada developed a points system for new immigrants; applicants were marked on employment skills, educational background, work experience and language skills. Gurcharan and Jiti were well educated and spoke English, making them attractive candidates for immigration, even though most Canadian immigrants were arriving from European nations at the time. By 2010, China, India and the Philippines were providing the majority of Canadian immigrants.

Gurcharan's early encounter with the man who became his first Canadian boss started off poorly. Douglas Johnston, owner of trucking company Continental Forwarding Limited, met Gurcharan in February 1965. Since the newcomer didn't yet own a car, Johnston gave him a ride to the office for the job interview. Johnston's accountant was leaving the next day and Johnston desperately needed a replacement.

"I asked a lot of stupid questions because I was ignorant about India," he said years later. "I even asked him when he was going to look like a Canadian. It was a stupid question, and he hasn't changed to this day." Still, Johnston was impressed with the unfamiliar man sitting in front of him, and hired him on the spot.

"My understanding was that I would work for him, day by day, week by week. Any time he wanted to fire me, he could let me go. There was no other understanding," recalled Gurcharan. "Doug seemed to have reservations about the way I looked, but he was prepared to give me an opportunity to run his office."

The two men remained friends until Johnston's death in 2013. During his first year of employment, Gurcharan told his boss he might want to sell Continental Forwarding Limited because the company was not doing well financially. Johnston, who owned several companies, listened to him and sold it in 1967. By that time, Gurcharan had already secured other employment. Johnston helped Gurcharan secure his first loan, accompanying him to the Royal Bank's Selkirk Branch. The branch manager asked Gurcharan how much money he needed, but Gurcharan wasn't sure how much to request. "I didn't believe in borrowing because I had never done that. But I knew we needed to start a new life in Canada and we needed a home and a car."

The branch manager helped Gurcharan work out a budget. Gurcharan received the loan on the strength of his word, his educational credentials, and Johnston's personal recommendation. Gurcharan brought a Viva Vauxhall car for $1,300 and purchased the family's furniture from K-mart for about $350. The Bhatias remained in their rental home until 1973.

After a year, Gurcharan started looking for new positions and received an offer to work with Statistics Canada in Ottawa. Gurcharan didn't want to work for the government or move to Ottawa, so he turned the offer down. He received an interview with Quality Construction Limited, a housing company that built homes in Winnipeg, Edmonton and Calgary. David Friesen, owner of the company, invited Gurcharan to meet the entire management team. Twelve managers, lawyers and assorted staff members set up a panel to ask Gurcharan about his cultural background, job experience and education. Two days of meetings followed the panel session. On the final day of meetings, Friesen asked Gurcharan to have lunch with him at a local coffee shop. At the end of the meal, Friesen ordered one tea and two cups, and insisted on sharing the tea bag with Gurcharan to save money. He offered Gurcharan a position as controller of accounts with a salary of $10,000 per year and three months' proba- tion. Gurcharan would be in charge of all the accounting and finances of Quality Construction branches, stationed in the head office in Winnipeg. As they left the restaurant, Friesen told him that he would be starting work the next day. Friesen would be leaving for Switzerland in two days and he wanted Gurcharan to take over all the accounts.

Gurcharan's first assignment was to investigate the Edmonton branch of Quality Construction Limited. Something was not right in the Edmonton office, and the branch was losing money. Gurcharan boarded the plane for Edmonton a week later, determined to find out why the branch was doing so poorly.

———∞———

The numbers didn't add up. Gurcharan was determined to find the problem. He looked at the books and verified the numbers again. If his calculations were correct, the manager of the Edmonton branch of Quality Construction Limited was embezzling from his company.

Gurcharan had arrived in Edmonton the day before. He found the branch manager to be polite, friendly and good-natured, and they had enjoyed a lunch together. The branch manager took him on a tour of the housing projects under development. While driving past them, Gurcharan counted seventy houses under construction. The next day, he went to the office and studied six months of accounting records. He noticed the branch had ordered one hundred and forty appliances, double the number needed to fill seventy houses. He wondered about the discrepancy. Where were the other seventy appliances going? He asked the branch accountant for clarification.

"I just do what the boss tells me to do," the branch accountant said with a shrug.

Gurcharan discovered the company had been ordering double the number of appliances for some time. He noticed the branch had made cash advances to purchase land for future development. Some deposits were a year or two old, but there was no record of land purchases or refunds for deposits on land. Gurcharan was suspicious and phoned the land development company to ask about the status of the transactions. An accountant said the money been refunded six months earlier. Quality Construction Limited had no outstanding business with them. Gurcharan couldn't find any record of the refunds, so he consulted the branch accountant who informed him the money had been refunded to the Edmonton branch manager's personal bank account. Gurcharan investigated and discovered the company was missing $250,000. Gurcharan called the Royal Bank on Jasper Avenue and explained the situation. He asked if he could look at the branch manager's account balance and discovered the man had over $300,000 in his personal account. Gurcharan went to Quality Construction Limited's lawyer and explained the situation. His main goal was to get the company money back without involving authorities. Gurcharan and the lawyer contacted the senior branch manager from Quality Construction's Calgary branch to ask for advice. Then he confronted the Edmonton branch manager.

"Your scheme has been discovered. You need to just refund the money, so we can avoid going to the police and you can avoid going to jail," said Gurcharan. The branch manager returned the money. Senior management fired the branch manager and phoned David Friesen in

Switzerland to give him an update. Friesen was angry and frustrated because the Edmonton branch manager had been his favourite employee and he had never suspected him.

"Do you want to rehire him?" asked Gurcharan.

Friesen wisely refused. He appreciated the way Gurcharan had handled the situation and gave him a promotion. Gurcharan became vice-president of finance and administration for Quality Construction Limited, with an annual salary of $40,000 and a $2,000 bonus. Gurcharan cancelled the orders for the duplicate appliances, which had never been paid for. The branch manager had ordered the appliances and then returned the extra units, depositing the refund money into his personal bank account. No one at the Edmonton branch had suspected their manager since he was friendly and easygoing. Gurcharan discovered lazy accounting practices in the branch that had enabled the embezzling. He introduced a new system of recordkeeping and inventory control, and tracked all items purchased and acquired.

In his new position as vice-president, Gurcharan developed good relationships with the entire company. He made his most significant contribution to Quality Construction Limited by changing the focus of the company from home building to general real estate development. Under his guidance, the company began investing and purchased land for development in Winnipeg, Calgary and Edmonton. Managers received bonuses, staff had good salaries and the company was prospering well into the late 1960s. Gurcharan became the branch manager of the Winnipeg office as well. The Edmonton and Calgary branch managers consulted him when they had problems in their offices.

David Friesen, president of the company, continued to spend a lot of time in Switzerland as he finished a master's degree and a PhD in business management. In order to earn his doctorate, he was required to write a thesis. Gurcharan had been working with the company for about five years when Friesen called him into his office.

"I want you to do me a favour," Friesen said. "I will give you a leave of absence from the office for one year. During this year, you will earn your salary. However, you will not be working in this office, but in my law office. You will be in charge of researching and writing my thesis." Gurcharan didn't like the offer. "Mr. Friesen," he said. "I don't even have to think about this. I can give you my answer right now. I will not do this. It's unethical and it isn't good on your part."

Friesen urged Gurcharan to reconsider. He offered to send Gurcharan and the rest of the Bhatia family to Hawaii for six months so Gurcharan could write the thesis there. "My answer is still no," said Gurcharan. "I am not going anywhere, and I am not going to write this thesis."

Gurcharan went home to Jiti, explained the situation and told her he might be fired. "I knew David Friesen was a very emotional guy who had trouble accepting the word 'no,'" he recalled. Friesen gave Gurcharan a week to think about it. At the end of the week, Friesen fired him. Gurcharan consulted a lawyer who advised him to file a lawsuit against Friesen and the company. In court, Friesen argued that writing about the future of real estate development in Canada was part of Gurcharan's job description. He denied asking Gurcharan to write his thesis, insisting the project was related to company needs. The judge dismissed the case.

"I learned one thing," said Gurcharan. "There is always another side to every picture." He went to his friends, told them what had happened and started looking for another job.

— ❈ —

Work occupied only a portion of Gurcharan's life during his early years in Canada. He was still devoted to spending time with his family and to creating a more welcoming atmosphere to South Asian newcomers in his new city. His appearance and clothing gave him the opportunity to act as a cultural ambassador and educator, even to children. The American television show, "I Dream of Jeannie," featuring Barbara Eden as a genie, was a popular sitcom from 1965 to 1970. One day Gurcharan was shopping at Polo Park Mall when a little girl approached him and asked him if he were a genie. She had been confused by his turban and asked him if he could grant her some wishes.

"I am not a genie," said Gurcharan, amused by the situation. "But I can grant you a wish if you'd like." The little girl replied that she would like some chocolates. Gurcharan granted her wish. He believes in using humour in both difficult and joyful times, but he is not quite sure how he developed his sense of fun. "Humour doesn't come from books," he says. "If something is funny, it is part of your thinking and your reaction to situations. I can't say specifically that it comes from this source or that source, but at the same time, it comes from the associations you have with friends and family."

Sometimes he suspects his sense of humour is a survival mechanism developed during the harsh experiences of partition. "If we didn't have humour, we would never have survived," he said. "You have to take life as it is. Basically, we were always thinking that there were challenges in life. We have to accept them and not get depressed or give up our efforts. Certainly this is an attitude that has helped me to grow, think and survive." Gurcharan enjoys wordplay. He has a detail-oriented mind and often notices subtleties, especially in the interactions among people. "You can find the serious and the humorous part of everything. I take everything seriously, but I know there is humour in everything, too."

Gurcharan and Jiti made many friends during their early years in Winnipeg. Gurcharan spent a lot of time reading and talking to others so he could learn as much as possible about his new country. He began to develop his interest in Canadian multiculturalism and human rights, although he was not as active in these areas as he would be in later years. Building his career and providing for his young family took up a lot of his time. However, he and Jiti did manage to create a community. Only about twelve Indian families lived in Winnipeg in 1964. When Indians encountered one other on Winnipeg's streets, they were quick to connect. No other Sikh families lived in Winnipeg aside from Gurcharan's family and his sister's family, but other Indians could identify Gurcharan as Sikh due to his turban. Indian families in Winnipeg came from all of India's different regions, religions and ethnic backgrounds. They tried to forget the ethnic tensions of their homeland and formed new friendships in Canada. Hindus, Muslims and Sikhs soon began socializing with each other and helping each other.

"Everything in Canada was different from India," remembered Gurcharan. "There was no store in Winnipeg that carried Indian goods. We had to buy our groceries at Eaton's because we had a credit card and they were the only people who would accept a credit card. The manager of the produce department was friendly and accommodating. He would consult Jiti on the kinds of fruit and vegetables to import. At the end of the month, he would give her a basket of fruit, free of charge, as a gift for her advice."

The Bhatia family made many changes to adapt to their new country. "When we arrived, we were wearing shoes with rubber covers so we didn't slip in wet conditions. Of course, we had to get new boots to deal with the snow and ice," said Gurcharan. The Bhatias went for walks in the winter, bundling themselves up in parkas, scarves, mitts and coats to trudge outside even on the coldest days. They made friends with neighbours and frequently visited their homes for coffee.

"We never felt we were not at home," remembers Gurcharan. "We were never really uncomfortable because we met friends and friendly people. People were welcoming to us. It was only when I was looking at jobs that I encountered discrimination. They accepted my job qualifications and my ability to do the job, but some people wouldn't take me in because of my turban."

At the time, the population of Winnipeg consisted largely of people with European or Aboriginal ancestry. "The white people at my work were friendly," said Gurcharan. "Eventually I started noticing human rights issues. There was discrimination against natives, against women and in the employment sector. When you read the newspaper, you started noticing discrimination. But there was an interaction between the communities in Winnipeg, and there was never a feeling that there was racial discrimination."

Gurcharan describes one experience in Prince Albert, Saskatchewan. A city councillor said to him, "When you walk down the street, people will look at you because they don't know who you are. They might never have met a black man or a person like you. It's curiosity, not discrimination. We want you to understand this, and we appreciate your effort to explain who you are and explain your values."

Gurcharan believed conversation was the best way to break down barriers. "After you talked with people and dealt with them for a month or two, the barriers between you and them just disappeared," he said. "You just become a normal person that they deal with every day."

Gurcharan and Jiti took it upon themselves to educate others about their Sikh background. They started visiting United Church Sunday schools to teach others about the Sikh faith. They thought it was better to talk to the children rather than the parents. Children were more open and would ask questions their parents would not. Jiti and Gurcharan were able to communicate with the parents through their children.

Gurcharan prefers talking and discussion, and believes this might have also developed from his childhood experiences during partition. He wants to try and understand people, and have them feel a connection to him. Educating people has more benefits than being aggressive about a situation. Racism and xenophobia are based on fear of the unknown. Gurcharan tackled prejudices by writing letters to the *Winnipeg Free Press* about his culture and specific Indian issues, such as the Kashmir question and how India differs from Pakistan. He remained interested in the Kashmir issue and frequently spoke about partition and its impact. He wrote letters to defend Kashmir and Indian leadership, and to encourage respect for human rights, different religions and cultures. Even though he was not directly involved in community activism during this period, he still had some level of activity and concern.

The Bhatia family and other new immigrants began to visit one another on weekends. People couldn't buy Indian food in Winnipeg because there were no Indian stores, so they would gather to share food they had purchased in India, Vancouver, Toronto or Montreal. As more Indian families immigrated to Winnipeg, the more established immigrant families decided they should host formal gatherings to celebrate Indian religious holidays and heritage days. Some of the new immigrants wanted to share their cultural backgrounds and religious holidays with the rest of Winnipeg's population so they could educate others about Indian culture. This became the impetus for the Indo-Canadian Indian Society of Winnipeg. The group celebrated the birthdays of various Indian deities and saints, and observed holidays such as Gandhi's birthday and festivals such as Diwali, the Indian festival of light. Hindus, Muslims, Sikhs and Christians participated equally in the Indo-Canadian India Society. The group began to collect a library of books about Indian culture, religions and geography. The first resource library of its kind in Winnipeg; it eventually moved from a group member's home to the community association office. In 1969, Gurcharan and several other Sikhsbegan to meet weekly and organized the Sikh Society of Manitoba. It held the first gathering of Manitoba Sikhs in the home of Professor Hari Kirpal Singh. By 1972, the population of Sikhs living in Winnipeg had increased to such a size that it was no longer possible to have Sikh gatherings in private homes.

On August 15, 1965, the Bhatia family welcomed, their second child, a son named Gurvinder. He was born on a Sunday. Gurcharan drove around town for part of the day, trying to find an open liquor store so he could buy a bottle of champagne for the doctor who had delivered his son.

After many years, the Bhatias knew they would never leave Canada and decided to become citizens. Gurcharan became a Canadian citizen on June 16, 1974. "Winnipeg became home, especially after we were settled and Gurvinder was born," said Gurcharan. "I had good jobs. Canada became home." The process was lengthy, so the Bhatias didn't apply for citizenship until they had been in Canada for ten years. Jiti became a Canadian citizen on October 7, 1975.

Gurcharan had a busy life, but his children don't remember him as distant or unavailable. He never missed a school awards night or special event. "Family life was important to him," said his daughter Priti. "My dad travelled and worked a lot, but I never felt he didn't have time for me. I always remember him being around even though he was working. It was a traditional home. He would go to work and come home, and my mom was always around during the day. Most of the families around us were like that, too."

Priti and Gurcharan played checkers and did yoga together. On Sunday afternoons in the summer, the Indian families would go to Winnipeg Beach or Assiniboine Park together. The event, known as the "family picnic," included about fifty people. Priti remembers that her father did go out of his way to teach others about India and Sikhs. "In everything he's done throughout his life, he's always tried to teach people about what his background means and that people shouldn't take offence. At times, I think he was the only one wearing a turban. He would stop and talk to people. We would ask, 'Who is that?' And he would say, 'I don't know, but they asked me a question.'"

At one point Jiti thought she should work outside the home, but Gurcharan believed it was important for her to be available to the children. Gurvinder played hockey and basketball and Priti skated and swam. Jiti started bowling, and Gurcharan and Jiti took up bridge. The entire

Bhatia family participated in the community, and the children learned the importance of hard work, education and personal success. Gurvinder said he and his sister were taught that achievement should never come at the expense of someone else. They should never become successful by knocking someone else down. The Bhatias understood they should work for the greater good of the community. Education would enable them to do anything they wanted. Priti and Gurvinder never questioned that they would go to university and thought of it as an extension of high school.

A pivotal incident involved Sikh identity and bullying. When he was in Grade Four, Gurvinder transferred from public school to St. John's Ravenscourt, a private school that focused on academic achievement. The other students in his class began to tease him about his turban. Jiti and Gurcharan met with the headmaster to voice their concerns. The headmaster began to talk to students, telling them that everyone was the same inside. He urged them not to judge others by physical appearances, but by their character. Many students who had originally teased Gurvinder became his friends and have remained his friends throughout his life.

Gurvinder said his parents were among the first Sikhs in Winnipeg; they expected to encounter a response. "If something is different, people tend to fear it, and if they fear it, they react accordingly," he said. He suspects his classmates had never heard anyone speak about racism before and believes the way his parents and the headmaster handled the situation made life easier for students of colour who attended the school after him. Some Indians may have decided to immigrate to Winnipeg because of their connection with the Bhatia family, he said. Many families benefited from the cultural institutions and strong connections the Bhatias and other families had helped to create.

When he moved to Canada, Gurcharan picked up a hobby that became a lifelong habit. He clipped newspaper stories and kept files on items of interest. He now has extensive files of news stories on education, immigration, citizenship, Indians in Canada, India, human rights and multiculturalism. Gurcharan's most recent interest is gender issues and violence against women and girls. He has also kept extensive archives about his life and his accomplishments. Unfortunately, Gurcharan lost a large portion of his collection when the Bhatia's basement flooded in 2004, but he hopes the remainder will be useful to future researchers.

CHAPTER 9

SUCCESS AND
SETBACKS

Gurcharan knew he wanted to stay in real estate. After he lost his job with Quality Construction Limited, he started a successful company and became a real estate executive. He never guessed this business venture would end badly and that he would lose everything.

In Winnipeg, Ken Cutts, president of Fort Garry Trust, and Kent MacKinlay, vice-president, asked Gurcharan to act as partner and general manager of the company, while they would continue as financial backers and shareholders. Gurcharan earned an annual salary of $10,000 with the newly-formed Bestlands Development Limited. Bestlands began its enterprise with the construction of twenty-seven rental townhouses in Selkirk, Manitoba. The government of Canada and the Central Mortgage and Housing Corporation had invited real estate companies to submit proposals to construct housing for low-income tenants. Bestlands Development Limited won the competition based on good design, sound financial planning and affordable rental rates. Federal support covered ninety per cent of the cost of the new development, which was a great success. Bestlands contributed to the rising skyline of Winnipeg with the construction of several iconic buildings. The company built Plaza by the Riverside, the first pre-cast building in the city located across the street from the historic Fort Garry Hotel. Twenty storeys high, the complex was built and fully leased within a year, a record for local construction in the 1970s. Bestlands constructed a hundred townhouses and won another competition for affordable rental housing. Gurcharan, MacKinlay and Cutts then built The House of York, a twenty-three-storey apartment building in downtown Winnipeg. It featured more than two hundred luxury suites for high-income occupants and is currently Winnipeg's downtown Sheraton Hotel.

Business was going well at Bestlands, and the company was making money. Cutts, MacKinlay and Gurcharan received an invitation from Markborough Properties, a subsidiary of the Hudson Bay Company of Toronto, to plan, develop and build a $100 million commercial project in Winnipeg featuring a hotel and shopping centre. Another building created during Bestlands' ten year period of success was the Bestlands Building at Winnipeg's most famous corner, Portage and Main. The building was completed in a record seven months and originally housed Manitoba Telephones, and the Winnipeg branch of the National Bank of Canada. Bestlands also built houses in the North Kildonan area of Winnipeg.

Business slowed down in 1979 as housing markets started to falter and real estate prices fell. Then the management team of Bestlands forged a partnership that would cost them their business. A Calgary-based company, Abacus Cities Limited, approached Bestlands and offered to buy both Fort Garry Trust and Bestlands. Abacus Cities was a client of the Bank of Montreal. The bank looked at the proposed deal and told the management team at Bestlands and Fort Garry Trust that the agreement looked sound. The three executives were compensated with small cash settlements. "We were to get shares from Abacus Cities. The lawyers prepared everything. Everyone thought it was a good deal that would result in several millions of dollars of profit for us," said Gurcharan. Doug Johnston, Gurcharan's friend and first employer, looked at the contract and approved it. "But now in hindsight, I remember that the payment dates were not outlined in the contract," said Johnston.

Jiti was the only one who was suspicious. "I didn't think it was a solid business deal," she said. "There was not enough cash up front, and most of the deal seemed to consist of sheets of paper and no money. But I couldn't tell them what to do."

Bestlands received one million dollars with promises of many millions to follow. The three business partners received promissory notes with interest on them. Unfortunately, they never suspected the deal was a fraud. Later Abacus Cities was found to have lied about its assets, using fraudulent financial statements to lure shareholders. Abacus defaulted on its payments to unsecured creditors, and the company was placed in bankruptcy. "All the promissory notes we had were less valuable than toilet paper," said Gurcharan. "We lost everything. This was a historic day for me in many ways."

The receptionist in the Bestlands office happened to be listening to the radio when she heard a news story about Abacus Cities. She ran into Gurcharan's office to tell him what had happened. Gurcharan phoned the bank and his lawyer, who confirmed the story. Gurcharan, Cutts and MacKinlay held a meeting to figure out what to do. They decided to gather as much information as possible about the situation and meet with their lawyers.

"I wanted to go home and tell Jiti the news as soon as possible, so she could hear it from me first," said Gurcharan. "I wanted to tell her myself so she didn't have a heart attack." He left the office and drove home, thinking about how he was going to tell his wife he had lost all their money. Gurcharan's thoughts may have been dark and troubled, but the day was bright and sunny. He drove past the Eaton's store on Portage Avenue and stopped at the red light, his car window open. As he waited for the light to turn green, he looked out the window and saw an armless, legless man selling a pile of newspapers. The man sat in the sun, smiling as people put their money beside him.

"What a lovely, beautiful day it is," said the man to his customers. Gurcharan was struck by the man's happiness and good cheer. The smile stayed with him. "I thought to myself, 'This guy doesn't have arms or legs, and he can't walk, but he is smiling and enjoying the beautiful day.' I wondered what was wrong with me. I have legs and feet. My body is in good health and I have a sound mind. I wondered what I was worrying about and waiting for. I wanted to see what was going to happen."

Gurcharan watched the man for a few more seconds and drove off. When he reached home, he told Jiti he needed to talk with her. She made a pot of tea and they sat down together at the table. Gurcharan told her they had lost everything.

Jiti looked at her husband. "I am not worried," she said. "When we came to Canada, we didn't come with a bundle of money. You made all the money yourself. We don't owe a dime to anyone. We have beautiful children. What are we worrying about? I am sure you will find something else to do. It will be fine. Let's be happy."

She was encouraging and calm, and she didn't once remind Gurcharan about her earlier reservations about the deal. Some of Gurcharan's friends, including Sham Joshi, Balbir Singh and Devinder Singh, tried to ease his financial problems. Each one gave him a cheque for $10,000. The friends said, "We want you to start a new company and this is our contribution. Your other friends will also be happy to support you."

Gurcharan thanked his friends but rejected the money. He wanted to reflect before he made new plans and took action. Many lessons he learned through this ordeal stayed with him. Whenever times get tough, Gurcharan thinks about the man on the street corner and how happy he was. At the time, Gurcharan knew the bad business deal would mean a departure from Winnipeg. He had played a significant role in the development of the urban landscape. Seeing the buildings he had helped plan and build made him proud and sad at the same time. He couldn't look at the Winnipeg landmarks he had created without remembering the process of building them. He had enjoyed the work, and now he wasn't involved in the sector. "These buildings represented a huge creation and a multi-million dollar empire," he said. "It was a huge loss."

Winnipeg's real estate market was slow by 1979. The economy had tumbled into a recession and he saw little opportunity in the city. Gurcharan began looking for new places to go. One of his friends, Balbir Singh Kakar, asked Gurcharan to move to Edmonton to join him as a real estate advisor. He considered the offer. Priti was seventeen years old and Gurvinder was fifteen. Both were students at St. John's Ravenscourt school. Priti was in her final year of high school and would soon enter university. As she was in a time of transition, the move would be easier for her. The headmaster was fond of Gurvinder, one of the top students at the school, and suggested that the boy finish his studies by boarding at the school. The Bhatias decided to keep the family together. Both teens had a hard time leaving their friends in Winnipeg. One of the reasons they didn't want to move to Edmonton involved the sports rivalry between the two cities. The Bhatia children were not fans of the Edmonton Oilers and the Edmonton Eskimos, and continued to cheer for Winnipeg's sports teams for decades after they left. Saying goodbye to Winnipeg was difficult, but all family members knew it needed to be done.

Picture of Gurcharan as it appeared in the Continental
Forwarding Limited brochure in the 1970s.

Jiti's picture was in the newspaper as she appeared at a Winnipeg
festival, showcasing some of the aspects of Indian culture.

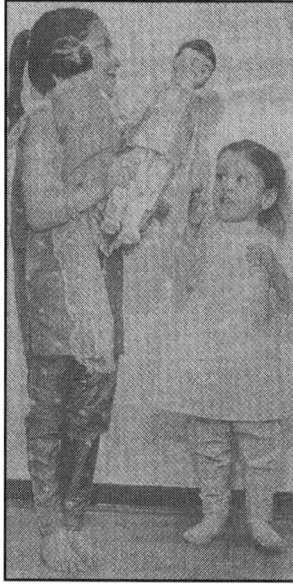

Priti, age 4 and Gurvinder, age 1, appeared in a newspaper photo as they
showcased some facets of Indian culture at a local Winnipeg festival.
The Bhatia family was always willing to teach
Canadians about India and Sikhs.

The House of York, one of the many buildings created by Bestlands.

The Bhatia family during their Winnipeg years.

EDMONTON

We need so much to work for coexistence, for tolerance and to say, "I disagree with you, but I will defend to the death your right to your opinion." It is only when we respect even our adversaries and see them not as ogres, dehumanized, demonized, but as fellow human beings deserving respect for their personhood and dignity that we will conduct a discourse that just might prevent conflict. There is room for everyone; there is room for every culture, race, language and point of view.

DESMOND TUTU

CHAPTER 10

A NEW PURPOSE

The teenagers were not impressed with their new home. In 1980, Edmonton was a blue-collar, industrial city that was just finding its legs. The city had grown quickly from 1940 to 1980, mainly due to rural migration to the city and European migration to Canada, but declining oil prices had begun to slow down economic growth. On the positive side, Edmonton was home to many immigrants, including a large Indian community and Sikh population. Even so, Priti and Gurvinder took a long time to feel comfortable in their new home.

Jiti was eager to move to Alberta because she thought staying in Winnipeg would be too painful. It took her some time to make friends in Edmonton, something she had done easily in Winnipeg. She knew the family would be fine, and she had faith in her husband's ability to come up with a plan and provide for the family. The Bhatias' quality of life never changed even though Gurcharan had lost all his money. A housing shortage in Edmonton had developed with the influx of newcomers. The Bhatias had to line up with three other families interested in buying the same house. They signed for it on the spot and moved into the four bedroom, two-storey house in south Edmonton, a home they have loved ever since.

Balbir Singh Kakar and Gurcharan worked together for four years. Gurcharan inspected, appraised and approved every property before

Kakar purchased it. Kakar expanded his business and bought property in Alberta, Ontario and the United States. The two men purchased ninety acres of land near Ellerslie in the south end of Edmonton; Kakar owned two-thirds of the land and Gurcharan one third.

Kakar stopped investing in real estate in Canada in 1985 and returned to India where he continued to build hotels and apartments. Gurcharan bought a group of townhouses in Edmonton's Beverly neighbourhood. The building's owner had cancer, so the real estate had gone into receivership. Gurcharan bought shares in the buildings. When the owner passed away, his widow sold the remaining shares to Gurcharan. Jiti became the manager of the buildings. The Bhatias borrowed money, paid off the loan for the property, sold it and were able to pay off the mortgage on their family home.

Next, Gurcharan bought the Allarco office building on Jasper Avenue. He purchased the four-storey building using a mortgage from the Bank of Nova Scotia, kept the building for fifteen years, and never made a profit from it. The real estate market in Edmonton was stagnant in the 1980s. The Bhatias had ongoing difficulty finding tenants or buyers for the building. In 2004, they sold the building at the same price they had originally paid for it. The new owner sold the building within six months and made a profit of a million. The next owner flipped it for a profit of two million. Today the property is worth about $12 million.

"Jiti called that investment bad judgment," recalled Gurcharan. "We should have held on for another two years." Gurcharan sold the land he had developed with Kakar. He had purchased the land for $3,500 an acre and sold it at $13,000 an acre after he had owned it for fifteen years. Kakar and Gurcharan never made a profit from the land, but the owner afterward sold the land for about $300,000 an acre.

Gurcharan was nearing fifty years old, and his interest in human rights was growing. His children were older, and he felt it was time to pursue other passions. He immersed himself in his new community and began meeting people and learning. He continued to work in real estate, but a newspaper called *Prairie Link* became his new passion.

When someone tells Gurcharan he can't do something, he often feels compelled to meet the challenge. At a community meeting, someone suggested the idea of a newspaper for South Asian immigrants living in Alberta. Gurcharan believed he had been dared to create it, and he decided to take on the project. "I think I have had a bad habit my entire life," he said. "I have always accepted challenges and lived with the results of these challenges."

The population of South Asians in Canada was still relatively small in the 1980s but Indian immigrants continued to arrive in the West. Before the days of the Internet, the newcomers relied on newsletters, letters and mail to find community news and connect with one another. *Alberta Link*, the newspaper created by Gurcharan, focused on the South Asian community. Many new immigrants had questions about settlement issues, immigration issues, and health care in Canada; they needed help to adjust to their new country and to Canadian culture. *Alberta Link* provided the answers.

When Gurcharan started the paper, several pessimists told him his publishing venture would fail. Others supported the idea and donated money to help the fledgling paper survive its first few lean months. To be viable, the paper had to develop relationships with its advertisers. They were interested in circulation numbers, and it took a long time to build the numbers. Gurcharan took on the role of journalist with enthusiasm. In the early years of the paper, he collected all the stories and did almost everything himself. *Alberta Link* was assembled in the Bhatia home and laid out on the dining room table.

As the paper grew, its focus changed. It expanded to include coverage of South Asians living in all three prairie provinces with correspondents in Manitoba and Saskatchewan. The newspaper's name was changed to *Prairie Link*. As the paper grew, three volunteer staff members helped Gurcharan collect advertising, write news stories and design the paper. Printed monthly, *Prairie Link* had a subscription base of twelve hundred households.

Gurcharan was still working in real estate, but his focus was on his new endeavour. He became involved with Indian societies across Canada so he could network on behalf of the paper. Satya Das, a former editorial writer for *The Edmonton Journal*, met Gurcharan shortly after he moved to Edmonton. Gurcharan had read Das' work and contacted him for support and advice. Gurcharan was particularly impressed by Das' article, "Multiculturalism, a kindly apartheid." The article argued against multiculturalism as tokenism and discouraged grants to cultural associations to propagate and perpetuate their own traditions, which might deepen the isolation of distinctive groups. Das' article was controversial and some readers of the *Journal* condemned his argument outright. Das and Gurcharan began to meet for lunch and discussion.

"At that stage, Gurcharan was in the transition stage of his life and his business," remembers Das. He believed Gurcharan's financial and business setbacks influenced him to change the direction of his life to focus more on community. "He still wanted to make a living for himself and his family, but essentially, he wanted to devote his life to public service." Das believes that *Prairie Link*, which eventually became known as *Canadian Link* when it expanded across Canada, had a larger influence than its circulation might have suggested. Gurcharan's skills as a connector, networker and promoter helped build the paper.

"Here was a man 'wasting' $30,000 or $40,000 to produce this paper," said Das. "It was a financial waste if you looked at it as something other than social enterprise. It was a brilliant, pioneering move. It brought a certain kind of inclusion and diversity to the forefront. Gurcharan's personal story and history had everything to do with it."

Das believes Gurcharan's purpose in creating *Canadian Link*, and the entire focus of his life after the age of fifty, was to change the attitudes of those in power, giving voice to those who weren't normally heard. He said Gurcharan understood that Canada was not a static nation: the country would look radically different in fifty or a hundred years.

Gurcharan never forgot his past and wanted no repeat of the violence he had witnessed in India. He wanted Canada to remain peaceful. "I knew I had entered business for a living, but at the same time, I thought I could play a better role- one that would be satisfying for me and my family, the community and the future, promoting multiculturalism, Canadian citizenship and human rights. That was my commitment and I carried it through. I am still committed to that."

Gurcharan was inspired by Das' argument that the Canadian version of multiculturalism seemed to focus on keeping communities separate, rather than integrating them. *Canadian Link* began to publish articles asking questions about Canadian identity and Canadian values, particularly as they involved newcomers to the country. From its inception as *Alberta Link*, the paper was published in English, as this was the common language of South Asians arriving to Canada. Gurcharan chose to print the paper in English so it would be accessible to as many people as possible. Ethnic newspapers were normally written in the language of the homeland, which meant that their audience was limited. Since *Prairie Link* was in English, it served a much larger market and could open a dialogue.

Satya Das guided Gurcharan in his endeavour, but he couldn't be too involved with the paper since he was working at *The Edmonton Journal*. Das was instrumental in giving Gurcharan advice and helping him out. As the paper grew, Gurcharan was able to step back and hire others to run the paper. He hired Beno John, a student who had several part-time jobs. John stayed at the paper for many years until he accepted a position in Toronto. As the paper grew, Gurcharan was able to hire people with journalism training, such as Allan Sheppard. John and Sheppard began writing all of the articles for the paper, leaving Gurcharan in the role of publisher and promoter. Jiti helped staff members assemble the newspaper, provided them with food while they were working, and solicited advertisements. Indira Puri, an old friend of the Bhatia family, eventually took charge of the ads and the subscriptions. Once the staff had prepared the page dummies, Jiti would take the paper to the printer, and the staff there would check that everything was in order. In the final step, Gurcharan would drive out to Leduc to check that everything was perfect before he gave the order to print. He was proud of his work, but acknowledged the venture was "a homemade paper" built of love and passion. As the newspaper grew, Gurcharan hired a full-time photographer and two staff members. *Canadian Link* established its own office space and operated out of a building on Jasper Avenue and 99th Street from 1984 to 1987. At one point, the paper went into bi-weekly printings, but this was too much work for the staff. The founders returned to producing one newspaper a month.

The newspaper evolved as new waves of immigrants transformed Canada into a multicultural nation through the 1980s. The question of how to integrate newcomers grew in importance as a political issue. Gurcharan's association with *Canadian Link* allowed him access to Canadian politicians he might not have met as a private citizen. Staff at *Canadian Link* interviewed politicians, and photographed them reading the newspaper, in a move Das called "cheesy as hell, but very effective."

Gurcharan used the newspaper to engage politicians, educate people and promote a vision for unity among Canada's diverse population.

"There was nothing harmful in what he was saying," said Das. "The politicians were relieved that they didn't have to take over the ownership of the debates because then they wouldn't get blamed. Nobody else was saying what *Canadian Link* was saying."

Gurcharan said the newspaper's purpose was to propose new public policy and to see its suggestions become public policy. "We wanted them to listen to us. How were we going to accomplish this if we didn't tell them our viewpoints? In a democracy, you have to talk and communicate. If you don't talk, how are you going to communicate and work together? You need to start bridging communities and start thinking like Canadians with shared values."

Throughout the paper's existence, Gurcharan networked and learned more about Canada's political system. He made friends with members of every political party and attended all the political conferences he could. These experiences led him to meet people who worked at newspapers all over the country, and he made valuable contacts. Even though he removed himself from daily operations as he became busy with other projects, Gurcharan remained dedicated to the editorials in the paper. Sometimes he wrote the editorials himself. In other instances, he discussed potential ideas with the acting editor of the paper. The paper continued to grow, buoyed by ads from major businesses and banks. However, *Canadian Link* was a non-profit undertaking, mainly run by volunteers, and its business model was not sustainable over the long term.

Indira Puri first met the Bhatias while all three were living in India. She worked closely with Gurcharan on *Canadian Link*, and moved to Edmonton from India in 1982. She had lived in Winnipeg and Ottawa in the 1960s and 1970s. A young widow with three daughters, Puri chose to move to Edmonton because of her close relationship with Jiti and

Gurcharan. The Puri family stayed with the Bhatias when they arrived in Alberta. As she was going to bed one evening, Puri noticed a copy of *Alberta Link* on the bedside table in her room in the Bhatia home. She picked up the newspaper to have a look and realized her good friend had started a newspaper. Puri was intrigued and excited by the idea, and she started volunteering at the paper. She learned a great deal through her experiences and said her involvement helped her come out of her shell.

Puri said she was an introvert who needed a big push. Working as the office manager for *Canadian Link* helped her learn how to deal with the public. She worked closely with the Bhatias and took over the accounts, finances and advertising for the paper. Both Jiti and Gurcharan helped her believe in her own abilities. Puri wrote an article about her experiences living in Canada and India and what it was like for her to shift between the two countries. After people read her article, they contacted her and wanted to talk about their own experiences. She never would have recognized her own talent for writing if Jiti and Gurcharan hadn't encouraged her.

Soon after she started working for the paper, Puri asked Gurcharan to explain the concept of multiculturalism. "He said, 'It's not just that there are lots of cultures. It's about what the government can do for different people coming from different backgrounds, countries and cultures. We have to talk about people's values and how these values connect us with each other. There are basic humanitarian values and everyone has basic rights.'"

By the end of its ten-year run, more than ten thousand papers were printed each month. Canadians in government, industry, education and the arts received the paper at libraries and cultural centres throughout the country. People in Edmonton could pick up the paper for free at the University of Alberta, the Edmonton Public Library and the Edmonton Tourism Centre.

In the early 1980s, the paper set up two foundations. The Multicultural Communications Foundation was a non-profit organization whose sole goal was to publish *Canadian Link,* while the Multicultural Education Foundation's purpose was to educate, hold meetings, critique public policy and arrange conferences to promote Canadian values. Germans, Chinese, Ismailis, Sikhs, Ukrainians and other South Asians came together with the common goal of teaching people about multiculturalism. The Multicultural Education Foundation promoted and organized national conferences in the 1990s and promoted *Canadian Link* to school boards, settlement agencies and political parties. The formation of the two boards allowed the paper to work independently. "We did not want the paper to stop criticizing the government about various policies involving multiculturalism while we were in the business of promoting multiculturalism through the Multiculturalism Education Foundation," said Gurcharan.

Both foundations had their headquarters in Edmonton, but their boards included representatives from across Alberta. The group held small conferences in the late 1980s and the early 1990s including a "Multiculturalism in the Media" conference. They led public debates and discussions as well as a forum on the International Day for the Elimination of Racial Discrimination. Group members conducted school visits and creative writing, art and music competitions for school-aged children. The Multicultural Education Foundation held a weekend conference to explore and strengthen relationships between multicultural organizations and Alberta's francophone community.

Gurcharan's goal was to strengthen a sense of equality among Canadians, whether they were born in Canada or abroad. He believed everyone should feel involved in the development of the country, able to preserve their culture and religion while participating in democratic processes. He hoped Canada could be a role model for the rest of the world because of its peaceful status and its multiculturalism. Gurcharan was an idealist, but he was aware of Canada's problems. Racism was the biggest human rights issue in Edmonton in the 1980s and Gurcharan was willing to talk about it, both personally and in *Canadian Link*. He noticed discrimination against Sikhs wearing turbans in the RCMP and against First Nations citizens wearing ceremonial head dresses. Challenging misconceptions, he focused all of his activities on education.

In 1982, under the leadership of then Prime Minister Pierre Trudeau, Canada introduced the Constitution Act and created the Charter of

Rights and Freedoms after two long years of public negotiations. The Charter was critical to the long debate over a revised Constitution because rights are easier to protect as when they are confirmed, written Canadian laws, rather than customs, traditions or assumptions. Under the Charter, Canadians who believe their rights have been violated can seek protection. Those who witness unfair treatment of others can act and ensure the rights of the oppressed. The Charter guarantees freedom of thought, belief, opinion, religious expression, peaceful assembly, freedom of association and freedom of the press. Citizens have a right to vote and can enter, exit and move freely around Canada. Over time, the Supreme Court of Canada has interpreted the Charter's guarantees to protect the equality of all citizens regardless of race, religion, sex, age, sexual orientation and mental or physical disability. Aside from these individual equality rights, Aboriginal peoples, women and cultural minorities also negotiated certain collective rights with the federal government; these protective clauses were added to the Charter's provisions and entrenched in the Constitution.

Gurcharan and Das had numerous discussions about the Charter. They believed it wasn't just a set of rules, but a living document meant to inspire people. The way to make the Charter of Rights and Freedoms relevant was to articulate it and embrace its inherent values.

Editorials in *Prairie Link* emphasized the Charter and its importance. Gurcharan believed multiculturalism needed to be included in the Constitution to reflect the diverse nature of Canada. His involvement with *Prairie Link* enabled him to have personal discussions with politicians. He believes these talks may have affected the way political leaders interpreted issues of multiculturalism and human rights. Laurence Decore spoke often with Gurcharan about his thoughts on the Charter. Decore was a prominent lawyer and city councillor who later served as Edmonton's mayor from 1983 to 1988, and as leader of the Alberta Liberal party from 1988 to 1994. During the constitutional negotiations, Decore consulted with Trudeau on aspects of the Charter, and Gurcharan believes his ideas may have influenced Decore's position. Gurcharan was proud to be part of the discussions, and he made sure *Prairie Link* was actively involved in the debates. At the end of difficult negotiations, the Charter included Section 27: "This Charter shall be interpreted in a manner consistent with the preservation and enhancement of the multicultural heritage of Canadians."

In the 1980s, people did not use the phrase "Canadian values" as often as they do today. According to Gurcharan, Canadian values include rights and respect for all living human beings, access to education, rule of law, justice and non-violence, tolerance, and protection of human rights as defined by the Charter of Rights and Freedoms. Canadian values include cooperation, the tolerance of ethnic and religious diversity, acceptance of new immigrants, and the ability to work cross-culturally. All of these values surface in Canada's institutions and in daily life. Throughout the decade, people tried to define Canada as the country's population increased and Canada achieved more recognition on the international stage.

Canadian Link tried to articulate the meaning of Canadian values. "In a way, I thought we were the authors of the phrase," Gurcharan said. "There are more than one hundred and ninety different nationalities, hundreds of different languages and religions in Canada, so we have a challenge to find out what connects everybody. And what connects us is our values. The real meaning of Canadian values was initiated during this time. Now every political party and politician uses the phrase."

Satya Das echoes his friend on the point: "In the early 1980s, no one else was talking about Canadian values. It didn't exist as an idea."

Marc Arnal, current dean of the University of Alberta's Campus St. Jean, met Gurcharan in 1984. Arnal was the director for the regional secretary of state in Canada, responsible for funding multiculturalism. The two men met when Gurcharan was looking for funding for *Canadian Link*. They liked each other and began meeting for lunch at the Mirabel restaurant on 109th Street. Their debates would often continue for two and a half hours.

"He had some great ideas and he was an inspiration in many ways," recalled Arnal. "He used to talk about Canadian citizenship a lot, in the sense he felt immigrants coming from other countries did not have an easy time figuring out what societal values were. He used to talk about portable and non-portable culture. I don't know many people who ever talked about Canadian values before he did. It wouldn't surprise me if he was the first ever."

During one lunch debate, Gurcharan explained why it was important to talk about Canadian values. When immigrants come to Canada, they have a hard time understanding the inconsistencies between their portable culture, meaning the culture from the homeland, and how to act in their new country. Gurcharan believed the silence and lack of discussion about Canadian values confused newcomers.

Arnal said Gurcharan has remained consistent in his visions and beliefs since the 1980s. "He's still singing the same tune," said Arnal. "He's a thoughtful man who is concerned about the health of the society he is living in. He doesn't just think about himself. He's a businessman and thinks about business, but he worries about how the country is evolving, the country's values and how young people are participating in it."

For the rest of the decade, Gurcharan busied himself with discussions about the changing nature of Canada, but he also worried about the growing unrest among Indian communities in the country. He felt so strongly about it that he was willing to face down a gunman.

CHAPTER 11

THE PEACEMAKER

The Montreal hotel room was full of Indo-Canadians of every cultural background, including a large number of Sikhs. In 1984, emigrants in the Indian diaspora were devastated and distraught about events in their homeland. The mood in the room was tense, and people refused to look at one another. No one spoke. The hotel staff was on high alert and had asked the police to wait outside the hotel in case violence broke out. Everyone knew the scene could turn ugly.

Robinson Koilpillai stood at the podium. The president of the National Association of Canadians of Origins in India was from Edmonton, a Seventh Day Adventist of south Indian origin. A Sikh extremist in the audience yelled at him, startling the tense audience in the room. The man claimed Koilpillai had called Sikhs "barbarians" in response to an attack on the Winnipeg-based Indian High Commissioner. The extremist wanted Koilpillai to apologize for his remark. Koilpillai replied that the man had misinterpreted his remark. Koilpillai had condemned the violent protest in the media, and the direct quote was: "People should not look at the violence done by a few members of the Sikh community as the actions of a whole community. The people who threw eggs and attacked the high commissioner and his car were committing a barbaric act."

His answer did not satisfy the extremist. The man walked up to Koilpillai and calmly showed him two guns resting inside his jacket. He told Koilpillai he was not afraid to use the guns. Koilpillai said he wasn't prepared to change his statement or opinion.

Koilpillai continued with his prepared speech. Other Indo-Canadians in the room waited quietly to see what would happen. Koilpillai was unshaken and his voice never wavered. The tension was palpable and no one dared move, as they were frightened someone would be shot. Some people in the room, like Gurcharan, had experienced violence in their past. They had seen more recent images of riots in India on television. They had watched as Sikh bodyguards murdered Indira Gandhi and violence erupted on the streets of India. Many feared the violence would spill over to Canada, polarizing the diverse Indo-Canadian communities.

When Koilpillai finished speaking, Gurcharan approached the stage. Sharma Padmanahbhan, a Hindu from Edmonton and a friend of Gurcharan's, said Gurcharan's actions that day cemented his belief that Gurcharan was a spokesman for the entire Indian community, and for peace and tolerance for everyone.

At the podium Gurcharan said he would give his speech in English and repeat it in Punjabi. "What has happened here is total anarchy and a threat to democracy," he said. "You have attacked a gentleman, Mr. Koilpillai, who has done more for Sikhism than most Sikh leaders. He has done so much that we used to call him Robinson Koilpillai. He has been a spokesperson for all communities and for multiculturalism. I feel ashamed to call myself a Sikh today. Sikhs have a history of protecting the weak and fighting injustice. I urge you to think about whether you want to be here, in Canada, and whether you want to be in this community or not. Those who do not want to be here have the freedom to leave," he said. And then he returned to his seat.

The meeting continued without incident. Afterward, Sharma Padmanabhan told Gurcharan he had a major impact on the peaceful outcome. The speech was an example of his courage and his leadership.

The movement for a separate Sikh state, known as Khalistan, began at partition when Sikh leaders were given the option to transform Punjab into an independent Sikh state. Instead the Sikh leaders chose to join India, remaining part of the larger, secular nation. However support for Khalistan continued throughout the years as Sikh extremists continued to agitate for their own state. The movement was strongest in the Punjab, with its Sikh majority population, but aspirations for Khalistan diminished as the Sikh community prospered and the Punjab became a wealthy state. Sikhs comprised only two per cent of the Indian population; many had influential positions in business, politics and government, and the military. Some Sikhs who moved overseas maintained their involvement with the Khalistan movement and sent funds to organizations in India to support Khalistan. In *Loss of faith: How the Air India Bombers Got Away with Murder*, Vancouver journalist Kim Bolan suggests that Sikhs abroad, particularly those living in British Columbia, were disproportionately drawn into the struggle for Khalistan in the late 1970s and early 1980s.

In India, Sikhs pushing for Khalistan engaged in violent action, resulting in counter-militant operations by Indian security forces. One such offensive was Operation Blue Star in June 1984. Led by religious leader Jarnail Singh Bhindranwale, the Khalistan supporters stormed and occupied the Sikhs' Golden Temple at Amritsar. The Indian army, led by Sikh general Kuldip Singh Brar, entered the temple to overpower the militants in a battle of Sikh extremists versus Sikh moderates, resulting in the deaths of a thousand people. Non-violent Sikhs were appalled by the battle and said the attack was a desecration of Sikhism's holiest shrine, while other Indians criticized the government for allowing the bloodshed to happen. Gurcharan said Sikhs were divided on the issue of Khalistan and on the principle of using violence as a means of control. "It was the most disappointing, stupid action of the government," he proclaimed. "Violence horrifies most Sikhs."

Gurcharan himself was opposed to Khalistan and frequently spoke out against the concept of an independent Sikh state. He believed that people who lived outside India no longer had the right to influence Indian affairs. He was also opposed to any further partition of India, as he had lived through its consequences.

"My approach has always been that the Sikhs had an opportunity, when India was divided in 1947, to demand a Sikh state then. The leadership of the Sikhs at that time rejected the option and decided to integrate their future with a secular India. They opted for a secular state rather than a religious state. The idea of the creation of a state on a religious basis was rejected, so the demand for Khalistan was too late and inappropriate."

In Gurcharan's opinion, the fight for Khalistan grew because of dissatisfaction with the Indian government's policies. "Violence was no way to demand and justify the creation of Khalistan. There were two different opinions in the Sikh community, and I belonged to the opinion which said violence is no means to solve any problem." He also believed the fight for Khalistan should not have been brought into the wider Indian or international community.

"This was a family affair within the Sikh community," argued Gurcharan. "I have always wanted people to sit down and discuss or debate to solve problems. I had a difference of opinion within the Sikh family, but I had no hatred for those people."

Unfortunately, the violence did spread to Canada. On July 19, 1984, Sikh demonstrators gathered at the Indian High Commission in Winnipeg, physically assaulting the acting Indian High Commissioner to Canada by pelting him with eggs. The Royal Canadian Mounted Police saved the situation by escorting the Indian envoy, Kalarickal Pranchu Fabian, to a private car. Angry Sikhs surrounded the car and pounded on it with their fists and sticks.

Prairie Link ran several articles against the idea of Khalistan. An editorial in the May 1984 edition angered the Sikh group Gurdwara Siri Guru Singh Sabha so much that they threatened to boycott the paper. The editorial declared that religious bigotry was the cause for communal violence and divisiveness in modern India. It directed Indians coming to Canada to leave their old battles behind. The Gurdwara Siri Guru Singh Sabha demanded a front-page apology in the paper and also wanted a personal apology from Gurcharan. They also urged other ethnic groups to join them in their boycott. The editorial wasn't directed only at Sikhs, but also mentioned the Hindus and Muslims who may have used money to propagate their religious beliefs to the exclusion of others. The article had warned against combining fanatical elements with religious, cultural and political activities. Gurcharan never apologized for his views or for writing the editorial. An article in the September 1984 issue of *Prairie Link* condemned violence in support of Khalistan and asked Sikhs living in Canada to stop advocating for Khalistan. This article also became contentious within the Sikh community.

Operation Blue Star wasn't the only political action that drew extreme emotions from Indians living abroad. On October 19, 1984, Prime Minister Indira Gandhi, daughter of Jawaharlal Nehru, was assassinated by two of her Sikh security guards. Riots erupted in India and more than twenty five hundred Sikhs were killed. As Canadians watched the news and the pictures of dark men with guns, some may have absorbed images of Sikhs as bloodthirsty, violent people. Many Canadians who had no personal contact with Sikhs may have thought negatively of them and developed stereotypes. Gurcharan wanted to dispel any prejudices people had about Sikhs. He wanted to let Canadians know that there were many people like him who were proud Sikhs and peaceful, hardworking members of society. He delivered an English version of the *Guru Granth Sahib*, the Sikh holy book, to the Speaker in the House of Commons so Members of Parliament could learn more about Sikhism. Gurcharan felt it was best to approach community members who were non-political and well respected, and whose voices would be heard. Representatives from *Canadian Link* and the Multicultural Education Foundation met with community groups, in an effort to promote better relationships between ethnic groups in Canada and to find opportunities to discuss Sikh militancy. Gurcharan advocated peace and spread the message that violence was not an acceptable way to deal with conflict.

"At that time, emotions were very high. People were not thinking in a rational manner. I was very upset about the attack on the Golden Temple, the holiest Sikh shrine. This was no way to eliminate extremists. It was just like an elephant trying to kill an ant."

Gurcharan was also upset by the negative media images of Sikhs as bloodthirsty, warlike, raving extremists. In order to counteract prejudice, he appeared on Sharma Padmanabhan's phone-in radio show and fielded calls for more than an hour.

"He was really in the hot seat," said Padmanabhan. He believed Gurcharan's message and voice were important during this time period because of his balanced view. Gurcharan was active and visible in Edmonton and in Canada as a whole. He is a Sikh, but he always speaks up as a Canadian and stands up for the community as a whole. There were a couple of incidents that made me sit up and say, "Oh my God, this gentleman is something else. He is bold in his convictions."

The Air India bombing deepened Gurcharan's concerns about the public's perceptions of Sikhs and Sikhism. On June 22, 1985, terrorists bombed Air India Flight 182, killing 329 people. Among the victims, 268 were Canadians, 27 were British citizens and 24 were Indians. As the largest mass murder in Canadian history, the investigation and prosecution continued for almost twenty years. Early reports identified the bombers as pro-Khalistan Sikhs who had been living in Canada. Inderjit Singh Reyat, a Canadian resident, was the only person convicted of involvement in the bombing, although many other people had been suspects. Singh pleaded guilty in 2003 to manslaughter. He was sentenced to fifteen years in prison for building the bombs that killed so many innocent people.

Sikh militant groups continued to agitate for Khalistan, waging an insurgency against the Indian government. The struggle continued until the early 1990s. The number of extremists and pro-Khalistan organizations in Canada has decreased significantly since then, but even today, some Sikhs around the world continue to support the idea of an independent Sikh state.

Gurcharan's ideas and advocacy were influential on a national scale because he was one of several Indo-Canadian men in Edmonton, including Krishan Joshee and Robinson Koilpillai, who were active in national organizations. Gurcharan believed his message would have merit in his homeland. In 1985, he travelled to India to meet with politicians to dispel myths and learn more about the political situation following Indira Gandhi's death. Some Indian newspapers were publicizing false information, saying that Canadians and the Sikh population in Canada encouraged Sikh terrorism in India. Gurcharan wanted to abolish these rumours. Documenting his journey in *Canadian Link*, he spoke with Sikh leaders, Punjabi government officials and members of the Indian federal government, telling people that Canadians did not support the violence in India. He spoke about how the actions in the Golden Temple had been detrimental and hurtful to the Sikh community in Canada. He expressed his sadness over the violence and told them Canadians stood for non-violence.

Gurcharan worried that the violence in India would spill over to Canada. He believed that communities and governments in India should resolve the crisis without Canadian assistance.

Later, Gurcharan made a deeper commitment to his community by joining new boards and community organizations. He became a director and the vice-president of the newly created Edmonton Immigration Services Association. This group, still active today, aimed to increase the awareness of immigrant issues and attempted to generate government and public support for the settlement of immigrants and refugees in Canada. The organization's members assisted new Canadians and helped them prepare for citizenship while promoting values of human rights, justice and democracy. The Edmonton Immigration Services Association has grown to become a much larger organization and currently employs about thirty people. Gurcharan's rededication to community service would be important in the turbulent months to come.

CHAPTER 12

WHY SHOULDN'T A MOUNTIE WEAR A TURBAN?

Baltej Singh Dhillon wanted to be a Mountie. Dhillon, a Sikh Canadian, met all the requirements to wear the red serge and tall boots of the Royal Canadian Mounted Police, but he confronted one problem. Dhillon could not don the traditional hat of the Royal Canadian Mounted Police because he wore a turban. The commissioner of the Royal Canadian Mounted Police, Norman Inkster, sided with Dhillon's right to wear his turban. However, the policies in 1989 required all RCMP members to wear a regulation uniform. Canadians who supported Dhillon's rights under the Charter of Rights and Freedoms pushed the federal government to change the policy so he could join the force. Naysayers opposed them. While denying they were racist, they offered endless reasons why a turban could not be tolerated. Some argued turbans would take away from the traditional image of the RCMP. Others said the Sikh head coverings were a safety concern, and expressed doubt that any man wearing a turban would be recognized as a Mountie. Others said officers could have accidents or become involved in fights and end up strangled by the fabric of their own turbans. More than 150,000 Canadians signed petitions to ban turbans from the Royal Canadian Mounted Police dress code. These detractors claimed Sikhs who wore turbans were refusing to be Canadians. Meanwhile, Sikh leaders and other supporters across Canada pointed out that Sikhs had worn turbans during service in the British Army in two world wars without any problem. Sikhs employed by Canadian city police forces and the Canadian armed forces already wore turbans as part of their uniforms. Still, the debate continued.

Many Sikhs were hurt and offended by those who wanted to ban turbans. They saw the reactions as a mix of racism, ignorance and fear. They called for people to think about the issue and the motives behind the banning of turbans. This wasn't the first time Sikh turbans had been a flash point of contention and discrimination. One early law in Canada had required Sikh taxi drivers to wear turbans that matched the colour of their cabs.

Gurcharan was one of the community leaders who defended Sikh turbans in the RCMP. He knew the controversy wasn't just about the turban, but about equality for Sikh people in Canada and racism. He was bothered by Conservative politicians who refused to discuss the issue. "Tomorrow they can go against Jews or they can say they don't want French living in Alberta," he told *The Edmonton Journal*'s Conal Mullen in November 1989. In April 1989, the RCMP commissioner recommended lifting the prohibition against turbans. On March 16, 1990, the federal Solicitor General, Pierre Cadieux, announced in the House of Commons that Sikhs could wear turbans while on active duty with the national police force. Dhillon became the first RCMP officer to wear a turban on the job.

Gurcharan was happy with the decision since he had advocated for the issue on a personal level and also as a newly appointed member of the Canadian Human Rights Commission. Gurcharan doesn't remember all the details about his 1989 appointment. He is not sure who recommended him for the commission. His work with *Canadian Link* and his involvement with various human rights community groups had increased his prominence and political stature. By this time, he was well known in communities across the country for his involvement with human rights work. People also knew him because of his editorials and commitment to the newspaper, and the foundations affiliated with it.

The Canadian Human Rights Commission meets in Ottawa once a month to review public policy and individual cases related to human rights violations. The Commission acts independently from the Canadian government, reporting to Parliament directly through the federal justice minister.

Gurcharan discussed the option with Jiti and then accepted the position. He thought the appointment would help him learn more about Canada and human rights problems while allowing him to express himself and his beliefs. His decision to serve as a commissioner turned out to be positive. It also increased his public profile. His appointment was announced in *The Edmonton Journal* and he received letters of congratulations from friends, politicians and other supporters. While he served on the commission, he was invited to speak at ceremonies and deliver speeches about human rights to community groups.

Max Yalden, who currently lives in Ottawa, served as the Chief Commissioner of the Canadian Human Rights Commission from 1987 until 1996. Later, he sat on the United Nations Human Rights Commission for eight years. Gurcharan served two terms on the Canadian Human Rights Commission, travelling to Ottawa monthly from 1989 to 1995. The Commission is comprised of six people at one time and includes two full-time commissioners and three to five part-time commissioners. Gurcharan was a part-time commissioner and was paid a stipend for his effort. Each month, commissioners received large binders full of cases. They had about four weeks to read and study each case, and prepare arguments before the two-day discussion meetings in Ottawa.

"Most people were conscientious about learning and reading what they were supposed to," said Yalden. "Complaints could be quite voluminous." Commission members would communicate with each other by fax or telephone between meetings. Due to the sensitive nature of the cases, everyone had to remain objective and discuss cases with great care.

Yalden said Gurcharan treated each complaint with care and thought. He saw him as a solid and useful commissioner: "He brought a different perspective to the commission, and it was important to have people like him on the commission. His perspective was different because he was of Indian extraction, he had different perspectives on race and ethnic discrimination and a broad view of life in western Canada."

He remembers Gurcharan as a genial person- a man who always had a smile on his face. "He had done well in Canada and brought an optimistic view of multiculturalism. He was very clear and fair in discussions, particularly when discussing complaints. He worked well with others."

Gurcharan liked Yalden as well, and thought he was an effective chairman. Yalden went on to push the Canadian Human Rights Commission to advance the question of Canadian Aboriginal peoples to the top of Canada's human rights agenda. He also championed the cause of Sikh applicants to the RCMP on the turban issue.

Gurcharan remembers many of the other contentious issues of the time period. Canadian banks continued with hiring practices that had not evolved to reflect modern Canadian society. Banks did not hire enough Aboriginal employees, or people from other visible minorities, to reflect their larger relative presence in the population; and the employers showed preferential hiring practices for white Canadians. Gurcharan played a considerable role in motivating the commission to meet with the banks to challenge them on the issue and to talk with bank executives about their hiring practices.

"The banks even made the excuse that they could not find many literate First Nations people to work in the bank. These people had fast turnover and didn't stay working in the banks for too long. I suggested the banks create an atmosphere that was more conducive to the presence of Aboriginal peoples," he said.

Gender equality was becoming more of an issue. Women still weren't hired at the same rate as men, and male employees outnumbered females in many offices. Women working in the federal government, the banks and many other federal institutions were not paid the same wage as their male counterparts, even if they were doing the same job. Pay equity was a hot discussion topic, and the discussion ultimately went to the courts.

"We didn't want to see the glass ceiling for women," said Gurcharan. "They needed to be promoted to higher positions as well."

The Canadian Human Rights Commission worked on many cases involving new immigrants who had been denied jobs because they had accents or their English was imperfect. The Commission ensured that these people were treated respectfully and financially compensated for their troubles. The Commission also handled cases involving ageism. Gurcharan remembers reading stories about female flight attendants who had been fired from their jobs once they got older. The Commission advocated for these women, enabling them to keep their jobs.

Gurcharan's appointment to the Canadian Human Rights Commission opened many doors for him. He attended conferences about employee discrimination and learned more about discrimination against women, visible minorities and Aboriginal people. Visiting different communities, and meeting so many different people, gave him a broader understanding of human rights problems across the country.

"It strengthened my resolve to promote Canadian values of equality and respect for other communities and religions, and to promote the Universal Declaration of Human Rights. I believe the Universal Declaration of Human Rights should become a guideline for developing future policies."

Gurcharan's work on human rights in Canada sparked his interest in global human rights issues. While travelling overseas, he attended meetings of human rights commissions in India, Australia and Indonesia. His involvement with the Canadian Human Rights Commission meant other commissions were quick to welcome him, even if he was not on official business. He thought it was important for Canadians to understand the situations of other nations, because this knowledge would help advance human rights in Canada, especially as it involved new arrivals to Canada. Understanding history and cultural norms around the world would help Canadians understand problems faced by new immigrants.

Gurcharan also increased his activity with numerous community organizations in Edmonton. In 1990, he sat on the Parks and Recreation Board for the City of Edmonton and helped encourage community groups and artists to apply for funding for various community projects.

Due to his increasing visibility and knowledge of human rights, Gurcharan participated in political dialogues, too. He joined other advocates within Edmonton's cultural organizations in the national debates surrounding the Meech Lake Accord and the Charlottetown Accord, two proposals at the centre of Canada's ongoing efforts to update the Constitution and to determine Quebec's status within Canada.

Gurcharan did not want Quebec to separate from Canada, but he opposed the Meech Lake Accord. He spoke against the division of Canada, recounting his own history with India's partition. Like other Canadians, he carefully watched events unfold after Prime Minister Brian Mulroney and the ten provincial premiers negotiated the accord at Meech Lake in the Gatineau Hills. Quebec had not approved the constitutional changes in 1982, so the Canadian government had gone ahead and made the changes without its approval. The prime minister wanted Quebec to accept the changes to the Constitution and the proposed five modifications to the existing Canada Act. One amendment recognized Quebec as a "distinct society." Other changes included augmented provincial powers with respect to immigration; provincial influence in the appointment of senators and Supreme Court judges; the right to a reasonable financial compensation for any province that chose to opt out of future federal programs; and the right of provinces to have a constitutional veto in the future. Because the Meech Lake Accord would have changed the Constitution, all provinces and the federal Parliament had to agree to its contents.

Many Canadians opposed the changes because they believed the Meech Lake Accord would create imbalances between provinces. Pierre Trudeau, who was no longer in Parliament, opposed the accord because he thought it gave the provinces too much control. He was very much a centralist and wanted the federal government to retain power. Liberal leader John Turner and New Democratic Party Leader Ed Broadbent supported the accord. The citizens of Quebec supported the proposals while the Parti Quebecois was against it. Preston Manning, leader of the Reform Party at the time, wanted the provinces to have more power, but didn't want Quebec to have special status. Many Canadians suspected that politicians had gathered together in secret to create the Meech Lake Accord; they were upset because they felt they weren't involved in any of the decisions. By June 1990, polls showed many Canadians also rejected the accord because of the distinct society clause for Quebec. The provinces of Manitoba or Newfoundland both rejected the accord, ending it as a potential compromise. Eventually, the accord was tabled. The debate over Quebec's sovereignty began again in earnest, and many politicians in all parts of the country joined the discussion on Quebec's place in Canada. Gurcharan was quick to involve himself in the dialogue. He appeared in a newspaper ad that explained why he had opposed the accord. The Meech Lake Accord brought the cultural communities into discussion with some of the thinkers and leaders at the time. It brought people like Gurcharan into contact with people who were thinking about Canada and its future, including Joe Clark and leaders of the First Nations communities. Gurcharan used his passion to try to convince people why the accord wasn't the right fit for Canada. His personal experiences strengthened his message.

CHAPTER 13

SEARCHING FOR SHARED CANADIAN VALUES

L ike other Canadians, Gurcharan watched the television news with alarm in the summer of 1990 as armed Quebec provincial police and Canadian soldiers confronted armed Mohawk activists. The Oka Crisis was international news, and it had a polarizing effect on the Canadian public. For seventy-eight days that summer, the Mohawks of Kanesatake, wearing masks and camouflage gear, blockaded roads, and refused to let the town of Oka build a golf course on their traditional land, including a burial ground. Land ownership had been in dispute for centuries. The Mohawks had filed a land claim, but the federal government rejected their case in 1986. When the town of Oka announced it was going to expand a golf course into the contested area, the Mohawks blocked the location. Quebec police stormed the barricades but were unable to clear the road. One police officer was killed during the action.

Residents of the nearby Kahnawake reserve supported the Mohawks at Oka by blocking highways across their reserve as well as the Mercier Bridge between Montreal and the south shore. The province of Quebec attempted to cut food supplies to the area, but the Mohawks called in the Red Cross for emergency supplies. In the end, the province asked the federal government to send in the army. Nothing was ever resolved, even after the standoff ended. The crisis divided the Canadian public and opened a new dialogue about Aboriginal rights and politics. In many cases, racist opinions dominated public discussion. The media reported the crisis by the hour, and Aboriginal people across Canada demonstrated in their own communities, in support of the Oka Mohawks by barricading roads and bridges. Aboriginal people from other regions travelled to Oka to show their support.

As a new decade opened, the demographic composition of Canada was changing rapidly. After 1990, Canada added about 250,000 new immigrants every year, compared to the 1980 levels of 125,000 people annually. Immigration became the main factor of net population growth. Newcomers from China, Vietnam, the Philippines, India, Pakistan and the Middle East now outnumbered newcomers from Europe and the United States. At the same time, the calls for full Aboriginal rights were becoming more prominent and there was increasing attention to gay and lesbian equality. Economic globalization became a dominant trend as international trade increased. Western Canada's population grew as workers from other provinces flooded into Alberta's cities and towns in search of jobs.

Gurcharan was still politically active and busy with various community organizations and the Canadian Human Rights Commission in the 1990s. However, he was no longer affiliated with *Canadian Link*, which had ceased publication. A lack of adequate financial support, rising publishing and distribution costs, and the changing nature of print media contributed to the demise of the paper.

Systemic discrimination against Canada's Aboriginal peoples continued to gain more attention with high-profile cases of police harassment in Manitoba and Saskatchewan. In November 1990, two Saskatoon police officers drove a seventeen-year-old named Neil Stonechild to the city's outskirts, leaving him to freeze to death in a deserted industrial area on a cold winter night. Stonechild had lived in Saskatoon, was not a gang member and had not displayed violent tendencies. His criminal behaviour consisted of underage drinking and petty theft. The officers arrested him for disturbing the peace and being under the influence, and chose to beat him and abandon him outside the city where he died. This case - not an isolated one, unfortunately- focused public attention on racism against Canada's First Nations, Métis and Inuit peoples. Stonechild's death, and the investigations of similar incidents involving other men, resulted in an overhaul of the Saskatoon police force and new acknowledgment of racism against Canada's Aboriginal peoples.

Throughout this period, Gurcharan continued to meet politicians and leaders from across the country. One of the people he met was First Nations leader Phil Fontaine who was Grand Chief of the Assembly of Manitoba Chiefs in 1991. Fontaine went on to become the national chief of the Assembly of First Nations in 1997. Gurcharan had one discussion with Fontaine in which they discussed Gandhian principles of non-violence. Fontaine later adopted these principles and proclaimed they should be applied to Aboriginal communities and their struggle for self-determination. He spoke at a Mahatma Gandhi Foundation event in Edmonton as a keynote speaker, promoting the way of non-violence.

The country's debates energized the leaders of cultural organizations, and they began talking about multiculturalism, the future of Canada, and Canadian values. To support the discussion, the Multicultural Education Foundation held the "Values and Visions" conference. The two-day event took place in November 1991 in Lister Hall at the University of Alberta. Participants discussed Canadian values and how the Meech Lake Accord and its fallout had affected communities in Canada. As conference chair, Gurcharan worked with Robinson Koilpillai and many others to organize the event. Guest speakers included Joe Clark, then minister of Foreign Affairs; Claude Ryan, a Liberal politician from Quebec who had led the "No" faction on the Quebec sovereignty issue; and Patrick Watson, then chairman of the Canadian Broadcasting Corporation. Jim Edwards, one of Edmonton's Conservative Members of Parliament for Edmonton, and Fil Fraser, Edmonton author and head of the Alberta Human Rights Commission, also delivered lectures. People in the arts, academia, business, media and multicultural communities participated in the conference to express their views concerning Canada's constitutional reforms. They discussed shared values that united Canadians and proposed methods to promote more harmonious relationships and national unity within a diverse country. Their goals were to determine the future of Canada, and articulate their dream for a Canada that was inclusive for all.

Gurcharan considered the conference a major success, with one shortcoming. Clark had promised the conference organizers some federal funding, but they never saw a penny of the $40,000 they had anticipated. As a result of the shortfall, conference organizers carried a debt and had to negotiate with their creditors. For the next three years, people affiliated with the conference held large, elaborate dinners and fundraisers to rid themselves of the debt. The experience was disheartening and embarrassing, and the financial problems were never repeated at future Edmonton conferences.

The country was still dealing with issues of identity and with its lingering political problems. The Charlottetown Accord of 1992 was an attempt to rectify the problems caused by the failure of the Meech Lake Accord. The Conservative government tried again to achieve agreement on constitutional reforms and held wide public consultations before the politicians had their own meetings. Federal, provincial, and territorial ministers and the leaders of the major Aboriginal organizations met in Charlottetown, Prince Edward Island to agree on proposals for change in a number of areas, including Aboriginal self-government and Senate reform.

As Canadians debated the nature and future of their country, Gurcharan and others held large conferences designed to encourage people to reflect and become involved in the discussions. In 1995, the Canadian Human Rights Foundation organized another conference called "Human Rights and Changing Global Values" in Edmonton. The conference was held once again in November, and its theme encompassed the Universal Declaration of Human Rights as well as the 1993 Vienna Conference on Human Rights. People who attended the conference discussed how to advance human rights values through international education and law. Gurcharan gave the keynote speech, which was titled "Challenges to implement universal values in 1995 and beyond." Max Yalden, Jim Edwards, Phil Fontaine, Joe Clark and Jack O'Neill, Chief Commissioner of the Alberta Human Rights Commission, also spoke at the event. Three hundred people came to the weekend conference and listened to panels on religion, human rights, and the Canadian constitutional debates.

"We were not interested in the referendum, but in people's understanding of what the proposed constitutional changes meant for different people, particularly newcomers, native peoples and immigrants," said Gurcharan.

These debates and political activities in the 1990s highlighted an evolution in Canada from a country composed of Aboriginal peoples, and citizens of mostly French and British ancestry, into a more diverse nation where one out of every five people was born overseas. Gurcharan and other leaders of cultural organizations were becoming more prominent and they contributed their ideas to the national discussion.

CHAPTER 14

FAMILY COMES FIRST

Gurcharan kept busy with public affairs, but his family life was always extremely important to him. His family continued to grow and change. His daughter, Priti, married Michael Laderoute on July 31, 1993. Michael is a triplet, a single brother to identical twins. He grew up in Edmonton and is a Catholic of French descent. Priti, who had already graduated from university with a bachelor's degree, met Michael in a hotel and restaurant management program at the Southern Alberta Institute of Technology in Calgary.

Priti remembered his first meeting with Gurcharan: "I think Michael was scared to meet him, but I think my dad was just as scared." She had brought Michael to the family home to meet her parents. Gurcharan was sitting at the dining table, visiting with family friends.

"Gurcharan has this thing," Michael said. "He always has a few minutes to sit and talk to someone and learn more about them. He asked me about my schooling, what I was going to do in the future and what my work prospects were." This was not an effort to grill a future son-in-law. During an initial meeting, Gurcharan will often ask people about their education, employment and family because he is interested in life stories.

"Whenever he meets someone, he tries to make them comfortable," said Michael. "He has lots of different facets to his personality and can fit them into many different situations. He can always find common ground. You can sit him down with a bunch of oil patch workers and he can have a conversation with them. He'll find a piece of commonality and be able to sit and chat. He can sit down with business leaders and have the same experience. He fits into whatever situation he's in. That's just his personality. He can talk to anyone, anywhere, at any time." Michael has noticed that most people seem to like and respect Gurcharan. "He doesn't demand respect, but you meet him and there's an air of respect around him."

After a few years of serious dating, Priti and Michael began to discuss marriage. By November 1992, Priti suggested Michael talk with Gurcharan about their wedding. Priti was living with Gurcharan and Jiti, so she went out one night so that Michael could meet with her parents in private. Michael called to tell them he was coming to have tea with them. He believes the Bhatias knew what was going to happen.

He remembers sitting at the kitchen table under a hot light, which made him feel like he was under criminal investigation. The lamp shone down on him during the entire conversation, making the situation even more intense. Michael kept a close eye on his future father-in-law, who played with a spoon while he talked. "I thought the spoon was about to go flying," said Michael. He brought up the subject of marriage and told Jiti and Gurcharan he and Priti would like to get married.

"It's very easy to get out of marriages here in Canada," Gurcharan told him. "Where we come from, it's arranged and it's a lifelong responsibility." Michael told the Bhatias that he and Priti knew marriage was a serious commitment. Gurcharan asked Michael about his parents.

"It was a long conversation and it went winding around for a while. He talked for a long time about the economy and how it was important that I get a good job. It was a little bit comical. At the end of our discussion, it was decided that the Bhatias needed to meet my parents and sit and talk with them. I think in an Indian background, there's the concept that the families are joining together, and Gurcharan wanted to cover all the bases."

Jiti wanted the young couple to talk about their different religions, communicate well and be open to each other. "In marriage, you have to accept each other and work together to become a family," she said. "When you marry someone, you don't just marry them. Their family becomes your family, too."

Both families wanted Priti and Michael to complete a marriage preparation course before their wedding. Priti and Michael found common ground between their families, even though one of them grew up Sikh and the other Catholic, and they have a strong marriage. Both the Laderoutes and the Bhatias are outgoing people with a strong focus on family. The Laderoutes and the Bhatias keep in touch. All of the Bhatia family loves Michael and believe he is the perfect partner for Priti. Gurvinder and Michael are also good friends.

Priti and Michael sent out a notice to announce their engagement. Their wedding was a fusion of their two religious backgrounds and included a traditional Sikh sangeet with singing. The couple was married in the Sikh gurdwara and held the reception in a hotel in downtown Edmonton. The Laderoute's Catholic priest married the couple in the gurdwara, saying that he was happy to perform the ceremony there because "God lives in every house." The couple's wedding blended words from the Catholic priest with a walk around the Sikh holy book. Hundreds of people came from across Canada and from India to toast the couple's happiness.

───── ∞∞∞ ─────

Both Bhatia children have definite impressions of their father and his character.

Throughout her lifetime, Priti has noticed the strength of her parents' marriage and the healthy home environment they created. "My dad is comfortable in his own skin. He tries to fit people into his life and get along with everybody. He is a curious person who appreciates young people, loves learning and always wants to ask people about their point of view. He might not agree with everything people say, but he invites others to express their own views. He's a big picture thinker who inspires other people."

The phone at the Bhatia household rings constantly; family and friends are always calling Jiti or Gurcharan. The Bhatias pride themselves on being hospitable. Priti remembers coming home from university to find her friends seated at the kitchen table, having tea or coffee with her parents. Now the children and grandchildren of Jiti and Gurcharan's friends come by for visits. Distant relatives, or the children of friends who are coming through town, will phone the Bhatias and stop in. They want their home to be open to everyone.

Gurcharan loves to learn from others. He likes to ask people about their jobs and the kind of things they like to learn and do. He continues to read newspapers, magazines and books, watch the news, read news online and write letters to friends and government officials. His daughter says he is good at keeping in touch with people and maintaining long friendships. Both Jiti and Gurcharan value the importance of hard work, and believe you can accomplish anything if you work hard enough. All Bhatia family members are skilled at identifying opportunities and finding ways to advance. Jiti and Gurcharan work together as a team, making use of their strengths and values. Jiti is the bridge-builder because Gurcharan can sometimes become completely focused on one of his projects. He sees the potential outcome, and can encourage people to become involved, but he often forgets that other people have their own needs. Jiti and Gurcharan consult with one other frequently. Like any married couple, they occasionally annoy each other. Gurcharan is focused on efficiency.

"If he has a job to do, he always wants to find the most efficient way to get it done," said Michael. "Jiti hates that. He's always saying, 'Yesterday you cleaned the house in two hours, so today, you should be able to get it down to one hour. That's what I do with my work, so I can get more done in a day.'"

Gurcharan and Jiti are among the founding members of the Edmonton Bridge Club. An excellent bridge player, Jiti plays two or three times a week. She's a better bridge player than Gurcharan because he tends to start thinking about something, gets distracted and loses focus.

Michael and Priti say Gurcharan rarely speaks of his personal accomplishments. This may be a family trait, because Gurvinder doesn't talk about his awards or accomplishments either. Gurcharan is more interested in his achievements in practical terms, wondering what he can do with an award and how it will contribute to his work and his goals.

"It's Jiti who is more excited. Gurcharan is very humble. It's just another achievement," said Michael.

Priti said her father has always concentrated on improving the world. His main goal is to discover commonalities between people and encourage them to live peacefully together. He has told Priti that he sits around with his friends, trying to figure out how to make the world better. Priti admires her father's moderate views. Some traditional Sikhs tended to be more militant, she says; they have tried to recruit Gurcharan to their ways, but he is not interested.

Priti and Gurvinder like to joke that they have trained their parents. "I'm sure there were lots of things we were doing as we were growing up that surprised them. We all worked together. I would bring my friends to the house and it got to the point where my friends would come over by themselves. I wanted my parents to be comfortable, so I brought people to the house."

Gurcharan's relationship with his son Gurvinder is a little more challenging. They have an amicable relationship and love each other, but they sometimes butt heads because they have similar personalities. Even Gurvinder's wife, Aimee, tells him Gurcharan annoys him because they have many of the same personality traits. Both Gurcharan and Gurvinder are dedicated workers who believe family and friends are important. They are creative thinkers who know how to push each other's buttons. Both have long fuses, but they are capable of losing their tempers, too.

"No one in our family is content with mediocrity or the status quo," explained Gurvinder. "Everyone in the family is always thinking about how they can improve things or achieve. My father's level of integrity is extremely high and it's apparent in all his dealings, whether he is working in business or interacting with family. This quality is something that does not change and never falters." Gurvinder believes his father is a practical and intelligent businessman, but Gurcharan was never solely interested in making money. "He's concerned with society, community and making things better for people. There's not a lot of compromise there."

Gurvinder earned a Bachelor of Science degree at the University of Alberta and went to the United States to earn a Master's of Business

Administration at Bradley University in Peoria, Illinois. He followed this with a law degree at the Washington University School of Law in St. Louis, Missouri. He returned to Edmonton to practice law with Snyder & Company and Parlee McClaws law in the early 1990s. He was a successful lawyer, but his true dream was to own his own business. He saw an opportunity in 1993 when the Alberta government decided to privatize liquor sales. Gurvinder had always loved food; wine was becoming a new interest. He noticed the development of chain liquor stores, and Mom and Pop liquor stores, and saw a niche for wine stores with a boutique selection. His parents still owned the Allarco building on Jasper Ave and 115th Street, and he decided to open his new business there in 1995.

Gurvinder continued to work part-time in law and left law completely in 2002. His store "Vinomania" became a great success, and he began supplying local restaurants with wine orders. He started writing for wine magazines and delivered wine commentary on CBC Radio and in *The Edmonton Journal*. He became a wine judge and travelled internationally, judging wine competitions. As Gurvinder became better known, people stopped referring to him as "Gurcharan's son." In fact, Gurcharan noted the transition as he became known as "Gurvinder's father." In recent years, people have started to learn more about Gurvinder's business and charitable activities, including his fundraising for Edmonton charities. Gurvinder travels extensively for work and is often out of town. This is frustrating to Gurcharan and Jiti, who would like to see their son more often. "My parents are mystified by my career, but they are proud and amazed," said Gurvinder.

Gurcharan clips his son's weekly wine columns from *The Edmonton Journal.* "I try to keep track of all of Gurvinder's activities, but I am no longer able to keep track of all his public relations," he said. He is proud of his children's many achievements, and supports them as much as he can.

CHAPTER 15

BUILDING BRIDGES BETWEEN CANADA AND INDIA

Citizens in the world's largest democracy were looking outward in the 1990s. India opened its doors to foreign investment in the new global economy and began to develop international markets. The middle class watched television and movies from abroad and started to expect the same amenities as people in western countries. The government of India had begun to sell state-owned enterprises in oil, power, telecommunications, banking and insurance to the private sector. Finance Minister Dr. Manmohan Singh guided the country's economic reforms.

India and Canada had many ties due to the many thousands of émigrés like Gurcharan and Jiti Bhatia, but other similarities existed. India's parliament and justice system were similar to Canadian institutions, making the subcontinent an attractive business environment for Canadian investors. The Indian legal system, based on British law, emphasized respect for contracts and private property. Many Indians spoke English, the language of business in the country. In 1991, the Indian government created a program to entice investment from Indians living abroad. People born in India or of Indian descent could own an enterprise in India while foreigners could own fifty-one per cent of a business. Gurcharan saw opportunity in these changes, and he had the perfect business partner to help him.

Jim Edwards, a former Conservative Member of Parliament for Edmonton South, first met Gurcharan through *Canadian Link*. The two men travelled frequently on the same flights between Edmonton and Ottawa; Gurcharan was travelling for his work with the Canadian Human Rights Commission, and Edwards for his political duties.

The former MP remembers being impressed by Gurcharan and his work with *Canadian Link*. "I thought it was an extremely laudable endeavour because there needed to be a two-way linkage between immigrants and established Canadians," he said. "I stress 'two-way.' The newspaper went a long way in doing that. What struck me at the time was not only his insight into people, and the foibles of people, but also his inexhaustible energy. He just has a remarkable depth of energy. He will be sitting there with a bemused look on his face and all of a sudden, he'll light up and say, 'I've got this idea,' and it's not a half-baked idea. He's thought it all the way through by the time he pounces on you."

The two men shared a keen interest in human rights. Edwards had served on the Alberta Human Rights Commission and had many of the same values as his friend. Edwards said Gurcharan has remarkably good business judgment combined with boundless optimism. He is able to read people and can easily spot people who aren't truthful or honest. "He won't reject the rascal or try to reform him, but he will relate to the rascal by sniffing out which buttons to push."

Along with eight Indo-Canadian men from Edmonton, Gurcharan and Edwards formed a company called East West Financial Insurance. Partners in the business had experience in business, real estate and insurance. They invested $10 million in capital in the project and were excited to act as intermediaries for anyone who wanted to invest or do business in India. East West Financial Insurance was Canada's first group of Indo-Canadians exclusively committed to financial, technical and industrial collaboration with India.

"I'm sold on India again," said Gurcharan in an interview with *The Financial Post* in 1994. "Reforms are irreversible and the country has enormous potential." Gurcharan and Edwards saw the most opportunity in India's insurance sector. The sole insurance company in the country was a state-owned insurance company, Crown Insurance, also known as the Life Insurance Corporation of India. It served only ten per cent of the population. Gurcharan's goal was to create a new life insurance company that would become a joint venture between Indian investors and an established Canadian insurance company. He also saw the potential for cooperation in Canadian and Indian telecommunications.

Gurcharan asked Edwards to become the director of East West Financial Insurance. He thought Edwards would become a great advisor and would lend credibility to the actions and activities of the company. First elected to the House of Commons in 1984, Edwards had been a parliamentary secretary to several cabinet ministers; he contested the leadership of the Progressive Conservative Party, coming third in the party vote that elected Kim Campbell. He knew people all over Canada, and because of his kind nature, he was nicknamed "Gentleman Jim." He lost his riding in the 1993 election that reduced the number of Conservatives to only two MPs in the House of Commons. Edwards was out of a job, but thanks to his good friend, his unemployment didn't last for long. He first visited India in 1993. Edwards and Gurcharan began contacting Canadian insurance companies Manulife, Sunlife and London Life because Gurcharan thought a Canadian insurer would be able to capture part of India's growing market.

"We thought it would be a good idea to go to India, meet some of the players in the government and private industry, and explore for ourselves," said Gurcharan. "It was not only a question of insurance. It was a question of Canadian investment in India."

In 1994, all ten board members of East West Financial Insurance Company toured India for three weeks to investigate investment opportunities. The Canadian High Commission supported the endeavour by helping the delegation coordinate tour details. Participants included Gurvinder Tuli, a real estate investor; Kuldip Singh Delhon, vice-president of an investment firm, and Narrinder Uppal, a professional statistician with numerous financial investments. Amar Singh, president of Bargar Evans Insurance -an Edmonton insurance firm- and travel agent Jarnail Sehra also joined the group. The delegation met with

Finance Minister Manmohan Singh in the federal government office in New Delhi. At first, the minister's secretary tried to delay the visitors. The Canadians had to promise they wouldn't stay long or take up the minister's time, but Singh himself was welcoming and gracious in his hospitality.

Gurcharan said to India's finance minister, "Look here, sir. We are allowed here for fifteen minutes. Your secretary told us you have too many appointments and we don't want to encroach. Thank you for the opportunity to meet with you. We will be exploring opportunities and want better business and cultural relations between India and Canada."

Singh smiled, called his secretary, and asked him to cancel all his appointments for the afternoon and order tea and refreshments for the guests. He told the delegation they could stay as long as they needed. The group spent more than an hour with Singh, who was very helpful. He encouraged them to examine the possibilities of life insurance in India and recommended several government officials who might help the delegation. He also told group members they could return and visit him any time they needed to do so.

In Delhi, the group met other local business people and members of the Chamber of Commerce. They travelled to Mumbai and met members of the Mumbai Chamber of Commerce in an attempt to find local Indian partners. Throughout their tour, the delegation met top business people and industrialists in different cities. Some people wanted to develop businesses in Canada. The delegation hadn't chosen to focus on Canadian government, but they tried to help the Indian investors so the tour could become a two-way exchange. The group spent nine days in New Delhi, four in Mumbai and four in the South Indian textile and tea-growing centres of Coimbatore and Ootacamund. They met business leaders at the Indian Chamber of Commerce and Industry at the Sundaram Hall in Coimbatore on August 17, 1994. The members of the East West delegation were impressed by the attitudes of K.G. Balakrishnan, chair of the Stock Exchange and Raj Govindarajan, an industrialist operating in Canada and India. The Coimbatore stock exchange suspended operations for half an hour to hold a reception for the Canadian delegation.

"We were told the stock exchange operations had never been sus-pended before, even when President Kennedy died. It was very interest-ing that they gave so much importance to our group. They were very hospitable." The delegation also visited factories, workers' housing, hospitals and cultural and religious centres, and they made over three hundred business contacts during the tour.

After the initial trip to India, some of the men left the company. Edwards and Gurcharan remained committed to the endeavour and set up an office in the Allarco building. Gurcharan was heavily involved in the company, but Edwards was the man on the ground. Edwards wasn't conscious of this at the time, but in retrospect, he saw his position as an example of his friend's business savvy. Edwards, a former politician in Canada, commanded a higher level of respect and business clout from Indian politicians who viewed all politicians, even inactive ones, with a high level of respect. Throughout his involvement with the East West Financial Insurance Company, Edwards made about ten trips to India and once stayed for ten weeks straight, becoming good friends with Minister Singh in the process. "It takes a long time to build relationships in India, but once you do, they're solid relationships."

In November 1994, Edwards participated in the World Economic Forum in New Delhi, signed representation agreements with several Indian companies and wrote a feasibility report about the possibilities of an insurance initiative in India. The East West Financial Insurance Company eventually worked with London Life Insurance of Canada af-ter the company expressed interest in the feasibility study. In March 1995, East West invested in Capital Trust Limited, an Indian investment bank in Delhi. The same month, East West participated in a thirty-two member business delegation to India, led by Raymond Chan, Canada's secretary of state for Asian-Pacific Affairs. Gurcharan did not partici-pate in that trip, but Edwards and a few other directors did. By then, Gurcharan had become the president of the East West management team, with Edwards as the overall president. The goal was for East West Insurance to take an equity position in an insurance project. They also planned to provide consulting services to encourage partnerships and information about industries in Canada and India.

East West Insurance bought three-and-a-half per cent of the shares in Capital Trust of New Delhi. Instead of certificates that represented their shares, the company delivered six bags of individual receipts containing more than 250,000 share certificates to Gurcharan. The group took this as proof that India desperately needed to modernize some of its operations.

By January 1996, the private sector in India still wasn't involved in insurance. That same month, Edwards and several other members of the East West Insurance team joined Prime Minister Jean Chrétien's Team Canada mission to Asia. The delegation included seven premiers and more than three hundred business executives and officials. The group attended the centenary conference of the Confederation on Indian Industry, which brought together more than a thousand Indian and Canadian business people in makeshift meeting areas in Mumbai's cricket stadium.

By 1996, East West Insurance had a five per cent stake in New Delhi's Capital Trust and had signed a memorandum of understanding to collaborate with the company in life insurance, leasing, financing and a Capital India fund. Members of East West Insurance hoped to work with their Indian partner to extend business and financial services in the country. They also wanted to help import Canadian products to India. But the efforts fell apart when Capital Trust couldn't set up their insurance arm and sold shares at a loss. When Capital Trust's chairman died, the company fell into a state of disorganization and transition.

The East West Financial Insurance Company venture ultimately failed due to changes in the Indian government. By the summer of 1997, the participants' optimism had faltered. India's federal government was a thirteen-party coalition government that included two communist parties, and progress on market reforms had stalled. The Canadian company had no financial agreement with any insurance company, and it was still trying to identify investment opportunities in India.

"We weren't successful for two reasons," said Edwards. "One was that the government of India changed and swerved to the left. The two main communist parties became part of the government and said they would shut the country down if the government proceeded with life insurance from foreign investment. And the Canadian partner, London

Life, was acquired by Great West Life, and Great West had no interest in India."

According to Edwards, Gurcharan was deeply disappointed when the larger Canadian insurance firms decided against involvement in the project due to uncertain government policies. The two men obtained legal advice on whether they should sue London Life, as they had invested a great deal of time and money connecting the company with India. In the end, Gurcharan decided not to sue and walked away from the project. Edwards saw his friend's decision as an indication of his remarkable strength.

The connection between the Edmonton delegation and Dr. Manmohan Singh continued, however. The University of Alberta awarded the future prime minister of India an honorary degree in 1997. Singh and his wife came to Edmonton to receive the degree. A delegation of local people, including then mayor Laurence Decore, greeted Singh at the airport. Edwards, Gurcharan and members of the Indian community organized a dinner to celebrate Singh's visit. To celebrate its connection with Singh, the University of Alberta established the Dr. Manmohan Singh Prize of $500 to be awarded to a student with top marks in Economics 213, a class that deals with the economics of developing countries. The Indian community provided the funds for this award. In later years, Dr. Manmohan Singh continued to display his fondness for Edmonton. Indira Samarasekera, the twelfth president of the University of Alberta, met with Prime Minister Singh while in India. The Prime Minister did not see British Columbia Premier Gordon Campbell, even though he was in the country at the same time and had requested a meeting. Gurcharan Singh Bhatia, Edwards and other members of the East West Financial Insurance did not regret their efforts, even though no investment plan came to fruition. They had appreciated the opportunity to try to grow Canadian business in India.

CHAPTER 16

THE HUMAN RIGHTS ADVOCATE

Gurcharan's son and daughter say that he would probably call the birth of his grandson or his five decades of marriage to Jiti as his greatest achievements; and yet in 1997, Gurcharan was awarded the Order of Canada, the highest honour for a civilian Canadian. He achieved the nation's recognition for his dedication to human rights.

The adventure started when Jiti and Gurcharan received a phone call from the office of the Governor General, informing them that Gurcharan had been nominated for the Order. Gurcharan was asked to keep the information confidential. He had to confirm his nomination by filling out forms that arrived in the mail several days after the phone call. Nominations for the Order of Canada are kept secret, and people generally don't know who has recommended them. All Canadians can be nominated and anyone can submit a nomination. Gurcharan's first employer and friend Doug Johnston was one of the people who nominated him, and he kept a copy of the recommendation letter he'd written. Gurcharan knew he was going to receive the award about two months before he attended the ceremony in Ottawa.

The Order of Canada, created in 1967, recognizes an individual for a lifetime of outstanding achievement, dedication to community and service to the nation. The Governor General presides over the affairs of the Order of Canada Council. An advisory council, chaired by the Chief Justice of Canada, assesses the nominations and recommends names considered worthy of appointment. People from all sectors of Canadian society are eligible for the three levels of membership; member, officer and companion. Each year, fifteen companions, fifty officers and a hundred members join the Order. Gurcharan is a member of the Order, celebrated for his achievements in promoting cross-cultural understanding at the local and regional level. His cultural activities in Winnipeg, work with *Canadian Link*, efforts with the Canadian Human Rights Commission and ongoing work with human rights groups and cultural organizations impressed the awards committee.

"When I heard I was going to receive the award, I felt honoured to be a citizen of Canada. I recognized it as a dual honour, because a person has to be nominated first, and then that nomination has to be approved by another group," said Gurcharan. Once they were able to announce the news, the Bhatias received many letters of support and congratulations from people in Edmonton, including the mayor, city councillors, academics and political ministers. Gurcharan was pleased to have his work acknowledged and recognized at the national level. Sandy MacTaggart, president of the University of Alberta, received appointment to the order at the same time. Jiti and Gurcharan and the MacTaggarts enjoyed their time together in Ottawa.

"We were thrilled to be in the distinguished company of so many learned and community-minded people who had made a great contribution to the development of Canada," said Gurcharan. Most award recipients stayed at the Chateau Laurier hotel where they were able to visit one another. The awards ceremony was held at the Governor General's residence. Honourees sat on one side of the room and their guests sat on the other. Names were called and the new members of the order received their pins and certificates. After shaking hands with Governor General Romeo LeBlanc, they signed guest books. The Bhatias enjoyed LeBlanc's company and had their picture taken with him. LeBlanc sent them an autographed copy of the photograph, which still hangs in the

Bhatia living room. After the ceremony, the award recipients enjoyed a reception with the Governor General and his wife. The Bhatias were thrilled to meet and speak with the High Commissioner of India and his wife. Gurcharan said his award served to remind him that he was a role model for both families and communities. His human rights work was far from finished.

—————∞∞∞—————

No one is sure who had the idea first. Gurcharan and two friends—Gerald Gall and Jack O'Neill—began to discuss the possibility of holding a large, national human rights conference in Edmonton. In 1997, Gurcharan chaired the Edmonton branch of Canadian Human Rights Foundation, which had its head office in Montreal. He was still involved with the Canadian Human Rights Commission as well. Gurcharan and Gall believed that a conference would be a good way to celebrate the fiftieth anniversary of the Universal Declaration of Human Rights. They wanted to hold the conference in Edmonton, but the Montreal branch of the Canadian Human Rights Foundation opposed the idea.

Gerald Gall cannot remember the first time he met Gurcharan, but believes they may have met because of *Canadian Link*. A professor of law at the University of Alberta, Gall specialized in constitutional law, human rights law and civil liberties law. He had served as a board member for the Multicultural Education Foundation. Gall died in March 2012.

Jack O'Neill was the third man on the organizing committee. A former Jesuit priest, he had served as deputy minister of culture in Alberta for thirteen years and was a chief commissioner for Alberta's Human Rights Commission. He likely met Gurcharan through his role as chief commissioner. He remembers holding earlier meetings about the fiftieth anniversary conference in an office in the Allarco building.

"Gurcharan said, 'We will have the best conference ever held in the province and country, with the best banquets and speakers.' "I didn't say anything out loud because I didn't know Gurcharan well enough at the time," said O'Neill. I agreed with the whole idea of celebrating it in one form or another."

Around this time, Gurcharan suggested Desmond Tutu should be the keynote speaker. The other men thought Tutu was a good choice because he would attract national attention and increase attendance at the conference. Once the three men agreed to organize the conference, they set about recruiting others who were passionate about human rights. They didn't have any trouble finding people who wanted to help them.

Gurcharan has a knack for finding people to volunteer with him or work on his projects. It might be his skills in negotiation, his infectious nature or his sheer conviction that his ideas speak to people. People always want to help him, even though they frequently take on more responsibilities than they can realistically handle because he is so convincing and compelling in his vision of what needs to be done.

"People want to join me because they care and want to help. For me, trust is the key thing, and your own personal example is important. People believe in the issues. They live in this world and watch every day what happens. They are touched by the desire for change. They want change for betterment, peace, good quality of life and human rights. They think they are doing it for themselves and the community, as well." He thinks his actions, and his own passion and drive, make people want to work with him. "You have to let people believe in what you are doing and what you believe in. That's very important. You have to practice what you preach or people will never trust you," he said.

Gurcharan believes people join him in his causes because they believe in what he is doing. They see problems in the world and they want to create a better future and a better Canada for themselves and their families.

The International Conference to Celebrate the Fiftieth Anniversary of the United Nations Universal Declaration of Human Rights was held at the Shaw Conference centre from November 26 -28, 1998. Newspaper articles about the event emphasized the religious differences between the three main organizers. Gurcharan was a Sikh, O'Neill a Christian, and Gall Jewish. This was in line with the theme of the conference, honouring the diversity of humanity. The gathering celebrated the idea that every single person is worthy of human rights, regardless of race, religion, culture or economic background. The three organizers, who became known as the trio, believed it was necessary to host the conference in Canada because the author of the Universal Declaration of Human Rights had been a Canadian. John Humphrey of Montreal had helped to draft the final version of the historic document.

"This conference was not just a conference," recalled Gall. "This was a happening and an event. It was the biggest human rights conference in Canadian history."

The trio set up an office in the Allarco building. Support staff joined them later. As the conference date approached and volunteer numbers soared, the group occupied seven offices in the building, which had few renters at the time. The Alberta Human Rights Commission, and representatives of other non-governmental organizations, met almost every week to make decisions related to the conference. As the conference date approached, the trio met daily with representatives from fifteen different conference committees. More than two hundred people helped organize the conference.

"We got very enthused about the project and we got other people to be enthused," remembered Gall. "This is one of Gurcharan's greatest strengths. He is an ideas person who inspires others."

Gurcharan attributes part of the event's success to the close coordination of the trio, as well as the volunteer and community support. "They were falling over each other to try to volunteer," said Gall. "It was both heart-warming and encouraging."

Gall and Gurcharan worked well together, but Gall admitted Gurcharan can be difficult to work for because he delegates a lot. "You can have a conversation with him and your to-do list has gone from zero to ten." O'Neill and Gurcharan sometimes clashed, pushing Gall to act as peacemaker. Gall believes disagreements occurred because the three of them were working closely together on a high profile event.

"There were occasional conflicts," said O'Neill. "Gurcharan would want something to be done and I would act as naysayer. Gurcharan is a visionary, but he sometimes doesn't see the whole picture. Sometimes he believes so heavily in a cause that he misses details."

Early on in the conference planning, people suggested names for keynote speakers. The trio decided to invite Mary Robinson, former president of Ireland; Antonio Lamer, then a Chief Justice of Canada, and Desmond Tutu, the internationally acclaimed anti-apartheid activist from South Africa. Each member of the trio decided to approach a speaker. O'Neil, of Irish descent, decided to contact Mary Robinson. Gall used his law background to pursue Antonio Lamer, and Gurcharan set off to acquire a confirmation from Desmond Tutu.

———— ◌◌◌ ————

In 1997, Gurcharan began flying to Calgary for lunch. He would enjoy a snack or coffee in the airport, three hundred kilometres away from home, then he would board the plane and fly back to Edmonton. His unusual choice of lunch venue helped him secure a special travel deal available to anyone who made forty trips on Air Canada. Once the trips had been completed, the traveller received two free round-the-world trips from the airline. In order to obtain his international tickets, Gurcharan flew back and forth to Calgary twenty times. He woke up early in the morning, drove to the airport, flew to Calgary and then flew home. His friend Dr. Madhu Bamhambani and his wife Sundri often accompanied Gurcharan on these trips. Whenever they were getting ready to fly, Bahambani would call Gurcharan and ask him if he wanted to have lunch in Calgary.

Gurcharan spent less than $2,000 on flights between Calgary and Edmonton and collected two business class tickets with a total value between $16,000 and $20,000. Air Canada has never repeated this offer.

Gurcharan and Jiti had big plans for their airline tickets. They would go to Capetown to meet Desmond Tutu and personally invite him to the 1998 International Human Rights Conference in Edmonton. But first they would take a vacation, travelling from Edmonton to Rio de Janeiro, and Sao Paulo, Brazil. From there they went to Igazu Falls, Argentina and Sydney, Australia. Then they went to Jakarta, Indonesia and Frankfurt, Germany, before landing in Capetown, where they stayed for two weeks. With a letter and phone call, Gurcharan had arranged a meeting with Tutu. He was determined that Tutu would be the conference keynote speaker. Tutu was an iconic figure, a living symbol of human rights and the anti-apartheid movement.

"He inspired the rest of the world and showed us that this kind of discrimination and racism was not tolerable," said Gurcharan. "He used the Gandhian method to promote non-violence, and the whole world accepted his views and philosophies. I had read that he was an excellent speaker and I was so motivated that I flew to South Africa to invite him personally."

Gurcharan was also impressed by Tutu's work on the Truth and Reconciliation Commission. He believed this process helped South Africa end the era of colonialism and apartheid.

"When Nelson Mandela was in jail, Tutu was the one outside, promoting the concept of anti-colonialism. He was the one fighting the apartheid," said Gurcharan. "The whole black community was angry about discrimination and the challenges it brought, including police brutality, segregation, and the extreme discrimination of one human against another human. Tutu was able to contain that anger and not let it become violent."

Born in Klerksdorp, Transvaal in 1931, Tutu was ordained as a priest in 1960 and eventually became the first black South African Archbishop of Capetown. He was an outspoken anti-apartheid leader, recognized around the world for his efforts to challenge the racist regime. Tutu received a Nobel Peace Prize for his anti-apartheid work in 1984. One of his greatest legacies was his role in South Africa's transition to democracy. In 1995, President Nelson Mandela appointed him chairman of the Truth and Reconciliation Commission to help investigate human rights violations that took place during apartheid.

Once in South Africa, Gurcharan had to pass many security staff and police officers who kept careful watch outside Tutu's office. Gurcharan was impressed by his hero.

"He was so welcoming and affectionate," he said. "When I invited him, he said he would think about it. He wouldn't give me a straight answer about attending, but said he would pray to God to help us make our conference a success. I told him, 'God would only be able to help us if you yourself make up your mind to attend the conference.'"

The archbishop smiled and said, "I wish you a successful conference."

"It won't be a success unless you come," Gurcharan told him.

After two months, Tutu confirmed his attendance. Jack O'Neill believes Gurcharan continued to call Tutu's office during this time to try to convince the archbishop to attend. Gurcharan was convinced it was the in-person visit that convinced the great man to come to Edmonton. "With the personal invitation, we could tell him how much the Canadian Human Rights Foundation West was involved with human rights activities. We could tell him the details about the conference and our activities. Without a personal meeting, this would have been almost impossible to explain."

The news thrilled the organizing committee. The conference became even bigger than before. Hearing that Tutu would be visiting Edmonton, the University of Alberta donated $25,000 to the conference. About nine hundred people registered to attend; hundreds more were turned away. The three-day event included fifty speakers and seven hundred delegates from thirty-four countries. Tutu was only in Edmonton for three days, but he took on a hectic schedule that included twenty-seven different visits and events across the city. This was his first visit to Edmonton, but it was so successful that he visited again in 2000. Gurcharan was present for several of Tutu's presentations in Edmonton and admired his humour, cooperative nature, grace and good listening skills. Tutu was also a great storyteller and was one of the speakers at the conference banquet. Jiti and Gurcharan were seated next to Tutu and his wife Leah Nomalizo Tutu during dinner. Other guests at their table included the president of the Canadian International Development Agency, the publisher of *The Edmonton Journal*, and the secretary general of Amnesty International. Fifteen hundred people attended the banquet.

Lois Hole, chancellor of the University of Alberta and later a Lieutenant Governor of Alberta, cried with emotion at the reception. She announced a $50,000 donation to the University of Alberta to create an annual human rights lecture. The lecture has run every year since 1998. Gurcharan contributed $5,000 to the start-up of the lecture series.

Ralph Klein, premier of Alberta, attended the conference. His participation likely inspired the Alberta government to accept the United Nations Declaration on the Rights of the Child, which it had not previously supported. In one instance, Klein and Tutu began to talk, and Mary Robinson joined the conversation. The trio became so involved in their discussion that they were late for the banquet's grand entrance. O'Neill believes that the three of them were talking about gay rights, a hot issue at the time. Gerald Gall remembers another key moment when

Chief Justice Lamer, Mary Robinson and Tutu were all on stage at one time. "It was unprecedented," he said.

The conference included numerous panels and lectures featuring international human rights advocates. Participants discussed the impact of the Universal Declaration of Human Rights and its meaning, as well as gay and lesbian rights, indigenous rights, globalization, poverty and the challenge of ensuring human rights for all humanity in the coming years. Lectures from the conference were subsequently published by the University of Alberta Press in a book entitled *Peace, Justice and Freedom*. Various levels of government supported this endeavour. The conference brochure included greetings from Kofi Annan, then Secretary General of the United Nations, and Prime Minister Jean Chrétien. Local, provincial and national media covered the proceedings.

Interested people filled the lectures and banquet halls. Human rights advocates included Romeo Dallaire, who had been Force Commander for the United Nations peacekeeping group in Rwanda; federal Justice Minister Anne McLellan; and Foreign Minister Lloyd Axworthy. Not everyone at the conference had such a high profile in Canada. Chinese and Vietnamese dissidents and advocates for the poor, disabled and disenfranchised attended as well. Young people had their own special youth session at Grant MacEwan College. On the final day of the conference weekend, Archbishop Desmond Tutu addressed more than twenty-seven hundred people at the Jubilee Auditorium in Edmonton while hundreds more watched on monitors throughout the city.

Conference organizers had invited Aung Sun Suu Kyi, Burma's voice for human rights and chairperson of the National League for Democracy in Burma. Placed under house arrest from July 20, 1989 to November 13, 2010, she was one of the world's most prominent political prisoners. She couldn't attend the conference, but managed to send a short letter to the organizers. The letter, smuggled to the trio through a number of secret connections, addressed the importance of human rights and the Universal Declaration of Human Rights. The fiftieth anniversary conference also raised the profile of human rights on the Alberta government's political agenda. The John Humphrey Centre, originally known as the Canadian Human Rights Foundation West, was created with the conference surplus of $100,000. The Canadian Human Rights

Foundation's Montreal office believed the Canadian Human Rights Foundation West was taking on too many of its own initiatives. The Montreal contingent had wanted to control the conference and host the fiftieth anniversary celebration in their city. Eventually, Gall, O'Neill and Gurcharan left the board of the Canadian Human Rights Foundation to create their own organization. Gall said the decision to leave the board and separate was painful. The western wing created the Human Rights Education Foundation and re-named itself the John Humphrey Centre, once Humphrey's widow had granted them permission to use his name. Gurcharan became the first president of the John Humphrey Centre; Gall was the second president from 2001 until his death in 2012. One of the John Humphrey Centre's major achievements was the creation of a booklet called "The Youth Guide to Human Rights and Freedoms." The federal government reprinted the booklet, which became the second most popular book written about the Charter of Rights and Freedoms. The conference itself was a phenomenal success, and one that people remember fondly.

"It was a landmark event for Edmonton," recalls Jim Gurnett, former NDP MLA, teacher and activist. "It was big and dramatic and on a national scale in a spectacular way. Gurcharan was proud out of his head to be a part of that. I think he floated around for a whole week after it happened."

CHAPTER 17

THE MEASURE OF A MAN

Gurcharan Singh Bhatia has a complex personality with many facets. When asked about his faults, he said, "One thing people tell me to my face is that I am always in a hurry. People think I am focused on some issue and want to get results fast." Gurcharan is able to inspire others by the sheer power of his passion. He is also skilled at spotting the strengths of individuals. He's a captivating speaker who can easily convince people to join his cause. "You need to be careful or you'll end up working for him," said Jack O'Neill.

"He's strong minded and you don't push him around," said Anne McLellan, a former deputy prime minister and Edmonton MP. "There may be some people who think Gurcharan has some level of arrogance, but these are the same people who think women who succeed are arrogant or pushy. People who know Gurcharan know he has the courage of his convictions. If he believes in something, he believes in it passionately."

Gurcharan's drive to succeed sometimes frustrates others. He prefers in-person meetings and sometimes gives long-winded explanations or speeches. Sometimes his speeches can sound like lectures. Gurcharan prefers a more institutional approach to his human rights work and likes to host conferences, hold meetings and form committees.

McLellan, now retired from federal politics, said Gurcharan would always invite her to events to speak when she was in politics. "I would have to say 'No' and he would not take 'No.' Sometimes my political staff would have to talk to him and he would try to negotiate so I could attend. 'No' is not a word that he understands."

Gurcharan is smart, open and listens to others. He may disagree with others' opinions, but he believes it is important to talk to people and stay current. He can be compelling and inspirational. "Audacious people, while they can be difficult to work with, can get things done," said McLellan. "They push boundaries and make things happen that wouldn't otherwise happen."

One of Gurcharan's trademarks is that he doesn't stay with one project, organization or goal for too long. He prefers to start a project, and then pass it on and go on to something else, once he has found someone competent who will maintain his creation. He always selects projects that have multiculturalism or human rights as their common themes; however, he only works on one project at a time.

Amarjeet Sohi, an Edmonton city councillor, and Jim Gurnett, former New Democratic Party MLA, both acknowledge Gurcharan's skill at convincing others to work on his projects. He takes a person for coffee, explains a project to them, and is so convincing and enthused that the person is unable to resist his offer. Several people said Gurcharan can be tough to work with, since he concentrates on the objective and forgets other people's obligations elsewhere. He can be relentless in the way he monopolizes the time of other people and sometimes needs to be reined in. This role often falls to Jiti. Gurcharan doesn't always realize that other people cannot be at his beck and call or respond to incidents as quickly as he would.

"I don't understand time management," said Gurcharan. "When I want to do something badly enough, I just do it. I find the time, even if it means I have to get up earlier."

Gurcharan's idealism works two ways. He is a visionary who wants people to dream big and accomplish great things, but sometimes he seems unaware that his ideas or dreams might be difficult to accommodate. "You have to set boundaries with him," said Paula Kirman, a community activist, writer and musician who worked with Gurcharan on a project in 2012.

Gurcharan's friends have noted his consistency in actions, values and beliefs. Douglas Roche first encountered Gurcharan when he was a senator. Roche, a former chairman of the United Nations Nuclear Disarmament Committee, author, parliamentarian and diplomat, was often asked to speak at the John Humphrey Centre. He refers to his friend Gurcharan as "the embodiment of reconciliation" since he overcame his tragic past and the violence he experienced in India to become a businessman and community leader who championed human rights.

"I've never heard Gurcharan utter a mean word against anybody, including the perpetrators who massacred his family," said Roche. "He's really a global citizen. He's a kind man who has triumphed in his life over adversity of the most horrible kind you can think of. That in itself is a message. It's not so much what he says, but what he *is* that makes his message so compelling."

Amarjeet Sohi came to Canada from the Punjab in 1981. He has never worked directly with Gurcharan, but has known him for about seventeen years. The two met at an event where Gurcharan gave a speech about the values Canadians share. Gurcharan talked about the importance of understanding Canadian history and the role Canada plays in international affairs. Sohi was impressed by Gurcharan's perspective on the role of immigrants in Canadian society.

"Gurcharan is an ambassador for true multiculturalism in Canada. He really understands multiculturalism from various aspects. His biggest contribution is his interactions with thousands of people. He's helped thousands of new Canadians swear allegiance to Canada and has helped them understand what Canada is about," said Sohi. He admires Gurcharan's collaborative approach and his contributions to the Indo-Canadian community in Edmonton.

"He's well known in the community and well respected. People go to him for advice," said Sohi. "It's important for people who come to

Canada to see someone who has been a success and has established himself as a practicing Sikh," said Sohi, who is also a Sikh immigrant. "Through Gurcharan's success, he has become a role model, even though that may not have been his original intention." Sohi admires Gurcharan's discipline and organizational skills. He believes Gurcharan's goal is to create inclusive communities. His view of Canadian values involves both individuals and the larger society. Moving forward, Gurcharan received an appointment in 1999 that helped him communicate his values and vision for Canada to thousands of new Canadians.

CHAPTER 18

JUDGE BHATIA

The Chinese applicant for Canadian citizenship was over ninety years old and had been living in Lloydminster, Alberta since she was twenty.

"You've been here seventy years," said Gurcharan. "Why is it so important to you now to become Canadian?"

The old woman spoke quietly. "When I die, I want to stand before God and tell him I am a Canadian."

She told Gurcharan she had lived her life as a Chinese citizen and now wanted to die as a Canadian. "I want my grandchildren to know I am Canadian." She smiled proudly and then started to cry as she was granted citizenship. Her family members cried as well.

It was an experience he would never forget, one of many in his new role as a citizenship judge. Gurcharan had received another life-changing phone call in 1999. When the person on the phone asked him if he would like to be a citizenship judge, he offered a quick reply: "I am not a lawyer." The judge on the other end of the line told him he did not have to be a lawyer and asked him if he had ever been to a citizenship ceremony. "I have been to citizenship ceremonies and loved them," said Gurcharan. The judge sent him more information about the position. The federal government appoints citizenship judges to four-year terms. They have offices in Citizenship and Immigration Canada branches across the country. It didn't take Gurcharan long to learn about his new roles and duties because he had been passionate about Canadian citizenship since his arrival in Canada. He served as citizenship judge from 1999 to 2006. "I loved every minute of it," he said.

"Judge Bhatia's background made him a natural for the Canadian Human Rights Commission and the citizenship judge position," said Anne McLellan. "He came here, worked hard and got involved in the community. He accomplished a great deal. That is important for new Canadians to see. It's important for people to see that the person swearing them in is, in some respects, like them, even if he has been in the country for a long time. He is like them because he made that traumatic decision to move to a new country."

McLellan's main interactions with Gurcharan happened during citizenship courts. "My most vivid memory of him is how much delight he took in those ceremonies. He had so much passion in explaining how he came to this country, what it meant to him and why new Canadians should feel passion and excitement about becoming Canadian citizens."

Gurcharan's past achievements, personal experience with immigration and Sikh identity made him an attractive candidate for the position because he exemplified Canadian multiculturalism. He has become known as "Judge Bhatia" to many. As a citizenship judge he was known for his elaborate ceremonies—infectious celebrations for new Canadians and their friends and family. He wanted people to understand his experience and how he felt about Canada, so people would share his delight in being a Canadian citizen. He wanted to impart the idea that Canadian citizenship was a privilege. Gurcharan wrote all his own ceremonial speeches, emphasizing his personal background. He called on new Canadians to get involved in their country and in their community. Gurcharan wanted to perform as many citizenship ceremonies as possible outside the citizenship court. He wanted to bring the event into community centres and school auditoriums.

Randy Gurlock, current area director for Citizenship and Immigration Canada in Edmonton, came to know Gurcharan through his work as citizenship judge. Judges do not report to directors of citizenship and are not public servants. They work in Citizenship and Immigration offices with staff, but report to the senior citizenship judge in Ottawa. This can make for a delicate relationship between judge and staff.

"Whenever you have someone in your office who doesn't report to you, it can be a problem. But with Gurcharan, it was never a problem. That relationship, which can be unusual, was fine with him. He was just great to work with."

Gurcharan reported to the office in the citizenship building several days a week to work with his administrative assistants who helped him arrange ceremonies, administer tests and verify papers and passports. One citizenship judge serves Edmonton and surrounding area, working from an office in Canada Place on Jasper Avenue. Calgary has two judges, and larger cities like Toronto or Vancouver have several. Citizenship judges must also perform ceremonies in the regions surrounding their home city. Gurcharan performed ceremonies in Lloydminster, Grande Prairie, Peace River and Fort McMurray. His territory ran from Red Deer to the Saskatchewan border. He also conducted several ceremonies in Yellowknife, Northwest Territories.

"Gurcharan has an approach to Canadian citizenship and a larger concept of citizenship that was really inspiring to people," said Gurlock. "He inspired the staff, me and new Canadians. He was really good at speaking about citizenship. When he talked about it, he was talking about more than citizenship in the legal sense. He spoke about responsibilities and being part of the community."

Gurcharan wanted the community at large to attend citizenship ceremonies and thought it was important for children to learn about citizenship. He liked to invite parents to the citizenship ceremonies held in schools. Gurcharan has a love for young people and he often liked to take a few minutes to ask children who were becoming citizens about their education and age. He believes young people have an important role in the country. "When we look to building Canada as a civil society, we should be looking to younger people who are responsible for building this society," he said.

Every person who wants to become a Canadian citizen has to apply to the federal office, where the RCMP verify their applications and then direct them to appropriate provincial offices. Gurcharan was required to review all applications originating from within his geographical boundaries. He also had to interview potential citizens to test their language ability, as citizens need to prove they can speak French or English. Following their language exam, applicants are tested on their knowledge of Canada. Gurcharan reviewed tests and checked applications before allowing successful applicants to take the oath of Canadian citizenship. If immigrants are denied citizenship, they can bring a social worker and a lawyer to plead their case and make an appeal. Gurcharan would then have to make a decision about their right to citizenship. His decisions could be appealed to the Federal Court of Canada.

Gurcharan often took the citizenship ceremonies out of the courtroom and into public places where Canadian citizens could witness them. He was the first citizenship judge to perform ceremonies at the University of Alberta. He held citizenship ceremonies at Hawrelak Park for Heritage Days and at the Edmonton Garrison for Remembrance Day. He invited prominent dignitaries to participate in ceremonies as guest speakers, according to the occasion. If it was International Women's Day, Gurcharan would bring in a notable woman to talk about women's rights. During Remembrance Day ceremonies, veterans would speak about the devastation of war and the importance of peace. Guests often included Anne McLellan, Senator Douglas Roche, Jack O'Neill and local journalists such as Paula Simons or Nick Lees. Over the years, many journalists in Alberta wrote about the special nature of Gurcharan's citizenship ceremonies.

In 2001, Gurcharan encouraged *Edmonton Journal* writer Nick Lees to become a Canadian citizen. Gurcharan's enthusiasm for Canadian citizenship convinced Lees, a British citizen who had been living in Canada for many years, to take the oath. Lees celebrated the occasion by writing a newspaper column about it.

Senator Douglas Roche said that Gurcharan's citizenship ceremonies were powerful. "It was wonderful to see a man who had immigrated himself and who had made such a contribution to the community. It was outstanding and continues to be that way. I found him an inspiration."

Judge Gurcharan Singh Bhatia always looked regal in his maroon turban and formal citizenship robes. The enthusiasm in his eyes and voice affected everyone in the room. Gurcharan spoke with conviction and authority. However, he did have one fault as a citizenship judge; he was prone to giving long speeches.

"His address, which was supposed to be about five minutes, would go on for about twenty or twenty-five minutes, even if it was hot or raining. Nothing got in the way of his Honour explaining that becoming a citizen was an important event, and they had made an important choice to become Canadian citizens," said McLellan.

In his speeches, Gurcharan often referred to Canada as "the best country in the world created by a nation of people who came from all over the world." Since Canada is a bilingual nation, Gurcharan had to learn how to recite the citizenship in French. Whenever he had to interview French speakers, he used the skills of an interpreter. Even though he speaks English, Urdu, Punjabi and Hindi, Gurcharan conceded his French is terrible.

On one occasion, Gurcharan gave citizenship to an Edmonton woman on her deathbed. Family members gathered around her bedside to witness the moment. She had lived in Canada for many years and wanted to become a citizen before she died. The woman had cancer and was only expected to live for another month. A while later, the woman's daughter called Gurcharan to say her mother's health had improved. She claimed her mother's happiness at becoming Canadian was responsible. Gurcharan awarded citizenship to more than 36,000 new Canadians during his time as a judge. Even though he hasn't been active as a judge for many years, people who received citizenship from him, often recognize him, and stop to talk with him.

Wendy Kinsella first met Gurcharan when he was working with the Canadian Human Rights Commission and she was the director of the Alberta Human Rights Commission. Kinsella was a city councillor when Gurcharan was a citizenship judge and she appeared as a guest during several citizenship ceremonies.

"Gurcharan has a real interest and commitment to citizenship," she said. "He didn't just want to make people swear an oath; he wanted to give to others. He didn't just want to have swearing in ceremonies. He wanted someone to come and speak."

Kinsella said Gurcharan is first and foremost a gentleman. "He is also a *gentle man* and is always caring, approachable and inclusive. These characteristics make him able to accomplish everything he does. He is completely without judgment. He can recognize situations and ways of coming to a solution. For example, in a conflict, his view is not to become angry and critical. His view is to become more inclusive and more of a gentle person."

Gurcharan's consistent message helped him to advance his human rights work, said Kinsella. "He makes you want to do better and be better. He's an example of how a person can solve problems not with violence, but with peaceful means. I don't think he's an overt pacifist; he just has a peaceful approach. It would never cross his mind to go on the attack."

When one judge retired, and a replacement had not yet been chosen, Gurcharan donned his robes and volunteered to administer several ceremonies until 2012. During Gurcharan's time as citizenship judge, he substituted for other judges when they went on vacation and performed ceremonies in Toronto, Vancouver and Winnipeg, travelling wherever he was asked to go. He remembers his time as a citizenship judge as a time of great joy. For him, it was an opportunity to share his love of Canada and what it means to be Canadian.

CHAPTER 19

AN EXPANDING LIFE

Students from every racial background and religion walked into the gymnasium carrying Canadian flags. Women wearing hijabs stood next to young Chinese men, while African women and Hispanic men followed behind them. The students, mainly new immigrants to Canada, were studying English as a Second Language at NorQuest College on Edmonton's west side. The group seated themselves in anticipation of their first Canada Day celebration. In the middle of the event, the master of ceremonies announced that several students would be receiving a special award: the Judge Bhatia Citizenship Award. When he heard his name, Gurcharan took the stage. The recipients of the awards came onto the stage and shook his hand once their names were announced. Some of them, like the tall man from Africa, towered over him. Gurcharan smiled at each of them, awarded them with the certificate and wished them each a happy Canada Day.

———<small>അളളെ</small>———

In 2002, Gurcharan became interested in NorQuest College, a post-secondary institution designed for adult learners who are taking full-time or part-time classes. The college has two campuses in Edmonton, and two in rural Alberta; it offers work experience programs and flexible learning opportunities. Gurcharan learned about the college when he held a citizenship ceremony on its campus. He was invited to attend Canada Day ceremonies soon afterward and has attended the annual celebration ever since. NorQuest has an outstanding program for students who want to learn English as a Second Language, as well as an overall focus on leadership and lifelong learning. Students who study English are generally between the ages of sixteen and forty; about sixty-five per cent of the student body was born outside Canada. The Canada Day celebrations inspired Gurcharan because of the multicultural makeup of the student body. When he attends a ceremony, he talks to the students and learns about them. He wants to hear what they think about Canada, as well as their issues and struggles. These discussions keep him connected to new immigrants. Gurcharan admires the efforts and mandate of the college and appreciates how the college courses teach international students about Canadian citizenship while they are learning the English language. "I see the world right there in the ESL classroom," he said.

He wanted to promote citizenship at the college and donated $5,000 to start an award. The college liked the idea so much that they decided to name the award after him. The Judge Bhatia Citizenship Prize was first awarded in 2004. Other funders donated $20,000 to the fund. The award is now administered by an endowment fund and is a permanent annual award for students. At its creation, the award was given to two students. Today, five students are awarded the $200 prize. Gurcharan himself presents the award to the students during the annual Canada Day celebration.

The Judge Bhatia Citizenship Awards are presented in front of a full assembly of about four hundred people each year. Recipients are recognized for their classroom behaviour, understanding of Canadian citizenship, and Canadian values. They have high academic achievement and are active in their communities. They are selected by their peers, so the process is both democratic and transparent.

Karen Faulkner, the Director of Fund Development at NorQuest, first met Gurcharan in 2006. He was one of the first donors she met when she joined the staff at the college. "Gurcharan's whole concept behind this is that if you move to Canada, you need to understand Canadian ways. We are a civil society and it's important that you're kind, courteous, helpful and all those things."

She sees Gurcharan twice a year when he visits the NorQuest campus. "He's always working on something and thinking of different ways to engage the community, with the intent of building a better society," she said. "His work is not for his personal recognition. This is work he has dedicated his life to. Every time he talks to me, he talks about how he wants to create a civil society. It's clear this is how he lives his life, day in and day out."

NorQuest College recognized Gurcharan's contributions by awarding him the college's first honorary diploma in 2012. The award acknowledges his relationship with the college and its staff. Gurcharan was given the award because he exemplifies the college's values of lifelong learning and passion for learning. He received the award in a special ceremony during spring convocation, held at the Winspear Centre on May 10, 2012.

Gurcharan continued to contribute to his community in various ways. In 2004, he was a member of the Visiting Committee for the University of Alberta's Faculty of Arts. In the early 2000s, he ran for public school trustee, but didn't win. Gurcharan won a number of awards for his work, including the Queen's Golden Jubilee Medal, the Commemorative Medal for the 125th anniversary of Canadian Confederation, the City of Edmonton Salute to Excellence Citation award, and a District Team Award from the Edmonton Public School District. He appreciated the recognition, but nothing turned him away from his true goal- working for people who had been victims of inequality.

"If humans are made to feel lesser, their self-esteem is compromised and they will never be able to participate fully in economic or social development," he said. Gurcharan's work has always focused on human rights and multiculturalism, but education has also been a strong component. Gurcharan knew the role that education had played in his own life and saw how it had benefited his family members. "Education is crucial to knowledge and empowerment, and will assist people to become part of a civil society." Even as he approached his seventies and eighties, Gurcharan remained committed to his own education- reading, writing, watching, joining community groups, and talking to others about their experiences.

⸺ ∞ ⸺

Gurcharan's family grew bigger when one of his favourite people was born. Sam Michael Singh Laderoute, his only grandchild, was born September 10, 2005. By this time, Priti and Michael had been married for about fifteen years. Gurvinder was not yet married. Gurcharan and Jiti had dreamed of grandchildren, but did not think it would be a possibility for them. Priti was incredibly excited when she told her father she was pregnant. The news thrilled Jiti and Gurcharan.

Born two months prematurely, Sam had to spend extra time in the hospital before he was allowed to go home. His parents and grandparents worried during this difficult time, but the baby rallied and he went home on October 28. Sam is the unofficial star of the Bhatia family and his needs are a priority for Gurcharan.

Priti, Michael and Sam live in a bungalow and they have no stairs in their home. When Sam was eighteen months old, he went to stay with his grandparents for a few hours. Eager to explore, the toddler climbed the stairs in his grandparents' house. When Priti and Michael came to pick up their son, they found an exhausted Gurcharan. Frightened that his grandson would fall, he had followed Sam up and down the stairs seventy-two times.

Sam loves cars, and his grandfather adores buying toy cars for him. The cars are not simple or cheap, but antique die-cast cars ordered from a catalogue. Each car costs about $25. Gurcharan has been buying these cars for his grandson since Sam was two. "He loves his grandchild so much," said Michael. "There isn't anything he wouldn't do for him. He wants his grandchild to run the country and be prime minister."

Gurcharan often talks to Sam about politics and shows him photos of the famous people on the walls of the Bhatia home. Like all members of the Bhatia family, Sam is active and involved. He takes swimming lessons, plays soccer and he golfs with his parents. Sam has a great relationship with his grandparents, known as his *nanni* and *nannoo*. He spends a lot of time at their house and even has his own room there. The Bhatias would love to have more grandchildren, but have accepted that this is not going to happen.

One of Jiti's main priorities is caring for Sam. She offered to take care of him full-time during the days, but Priti and Michael didn't want to do this. Instead Priti took a full-time job and Michael chose to stay home with Sam. The Bhatias fully support this decision and often talk about how Priti and Michael are good parents.

In May 2009, the Bhatias welcomed another family member when Gurvinder married Aimee Hill. Gurvinder and Aimee met while working on a fundraising committee. They were friends for several years before they began dating in December 2007. Aimee's background is in marketing and public relations. In February 2008, Aimee and Gurvinder went to California with other relatives because a good friend was celebrating a fiftieth birthday. Priti, Michael and Sam were there, and Jiti and Gurcharan came down to Napa to watch Sam. Priti told her brother it was time to tell his parents that he and Aimee were dating. Later at a family dinner, Gurvinder had no chance to say much during the meal. When Aimee left the room for a moment, Gurcharan said, "She seems nice."

"She is," said Gurvinder.

"Is this serious?" Gurcharan asked his son.

"I think it is," said Gurvinder.

Gurcharan smiled and said, "You had better hurry up, because we're not getting any younger."

Gurvinder and Aimee became engaged in Paris in April 2008 and married in May 2009. They had one small wedding with forty-six guests in Italy and a Sikh wedding with several hundred guests in Edmonton. Gurvinder wanted the big party and celebration and didn't want to emphasize the religious focus of the ceremony. His goal was to bring all the relatives together so that everyone could meet and celebrate. The Bhatias and the Hills like one other and get along well. In 2011, Gurcharan, Jiti, Aimee and Gurvinder travelled to India so Aimee could see the country for the first time and meet the extended family.

As he has aged, Gurcharan has had to tailor some of his activities. Most of his challenges began after he turned eighty. His hearing has deteriorated, and he is completely deaf in his left ear. He has a difficult time following the conversation in large, group meetings and prefers to meet with people individually or in small groups. He prefers to take a secondary role in meetings and organizations. He continues to be involved with the John Humphrey Centre, the Canadian Multicultural Education Foundation and various other organizations connected with human rights. He still gives speeches and lends his name and influence to projects.

Gurcharan stays busy and still believes in expanding his social circle and making new friends. He maintains friendships with people who have phoned him every month for years and has cultivated relationships with his friend's children and grandchildren. Gurcharan and Jiti go to the YMCA several times a week to exercise and have coffee with friends. One of Gurcharan's goals is to stay healthy so he can keep up with his grandson. Gurcharan still works in the mornings because this is when he has his best ideas. He spends this time drinking tea, reading newspapers and online news and planning before his meetings.

The family continues to visit India to see family and friends. The entire family used to go every few years while the children were growing up. Jiti and Gurcharan still like to travel to India when they can. They have recently started spending winters in Arizona, as they find Edmonton's cold winters hard to tolerate.

In February 2012, Jiti and Gurcharan celebrated their fiftieth wedding anniversary. The couple, along with Priti, Michael, Sam, Aimee and Gurvinder, travelled to a resort in Mexico for the celebration. Gurvinder hired a private chef for the event.

"You had better start planning our hundredth anniversary," Gurcharan said to his son. "It's going to be even bigger."

CHAPTER 20

DAUGHTERS DAY

The bombing of the World Trade Centre in New York on September 11, 2001 challenged human rights advocates around the globe in new ways. They had to confront increased religious misunderstandings, racial profiling, hate-based crime and violence, as well as a generalized hatred of Muslims and the Middle East among uninformed people. Gurcharan chaired the Building World Peace conference, organized in October 2006, as a response to some of these global changes. The goal was to encourage people to talk about the role of religion in creating peace. Douglas Roche and Senator Claudette Tardiff co-chaired the conference held at the Shaw Conference Centre in Edmonton. The John Humphrey Centre was a major contributor to the conference weekend. Participants talked about the way to promote peace and understanding of various faiths; religious leaders spoke on many of the panels. More than five hundred delegates developed strategies to educate against discrimination and talked about ways to increase cooperation among people from various religious backgrounds. The conference's advisory committee included more than forty people from Aboriginal, Jewish, Christian, Hindu, Muslim and Buddhist traditions.

Later, Gurcharan and several other associates decided to create the International Association for Citizens for a Civil Society. Formed on

August 10, 2010, the board of directors consisted of Gurcharan, Jiti, Satya Das, Mita Das, Allan Sheppard and Matt Beckett. The organization, which is small and not well known, wants to develop civil society in Canada. The group has a Facebook page and tries to promote its values online. The association has defined the five pillars of a civil society: a right and respect for the life of every born and living human being; the promotion of the rule of law, justice and non-violence; the advancement of literacy and education; the promotion of human rights and Canadian values, as exemplified in the Charter of Rights and Freedoms and in the Universal Declaration of Human Rights; and the advancement of sustainable economic development and respect for the environment. The five pillars of civil society help define the commonalities among Canadians and create a purpose for everyone who lives in Canada. A year after its inception, the Association for Citizens for a Civil Society began planning for its first major project, Daughters Day.

Gurcharan and some friends first had the idea for a day in 2011 to celebrate the achievements of girls and women. In recent years, Gurcharan had become interested in the plight of women around the world and began gathering newspaper clippings about female genocide and honour killings. Charan Khera, Didar Pannu and Gurcharan decided to hold an event called Daughters Day in Edmonton to bring awareness to gender issues. In order to fund the event, Gurcharan told friends about the project and asked them to donate $100 each to the cause. He was able to raise more than $6,000. The group presented their vision to representatives from forty local organizations in a gathering at City Hall in September 2011. As the year continued, local politicians continued to give their support to the project. Gurcharan became chair of the Daughters Day Committee, and Charan Khehra, a former senior economist and policy analyst with the Alberta government, was vice-chair. The organizers designed Daughters Day to celebrate the triumphs of women, while acknowledging the unique challenges they face. The province of Alberta was founded on the first day of September, so the organizers picked that day to celebrate the inaugural Daughters Day. They also picked that particular date to draw a connection to the "Famous Five," the Alberta women who had petitioned the House of Lords in 1927 to urge the court to accept women as senators. The name, Daughters Day, was chosen to acknowledge and recognize the idea that every woman is someone's daughter and a member of a family. The event started off with a broad concept and eventually evolved into something more concrete. In interviews with local media, Gurcharan spoke about how gender equality was an important component of human rights. Daughters Day emphasized the problems of people from developing nations, and countries at war, where gender equality was not always a priority. Pannu, Gurcharan and Khehra rallied behind the idea of Daughters Day and wanted to form a committee to plan a huge event in Sir Winston Churchill Square in downtown Edmonton. Paula Kirman, writer, photographer, musician and human rights activist, was one of the core group of people who worked on the first Daughters Day event. Other key people were Poushali Mitra and Sabrina Atwal, project director of the Indo-Canadian Women's Association. The Daughters Day group created an active partnership with the Indo-Canadian Women's Association. Jim Gurnett became the coordinator of the project in 2012. Gurnett had encountered Gurcharan frequently while working at the Edmonton Mennonite Centre for Newcomers and the Bissell Centre, but had never worked directly with him. Gurnett had heard about the Daughters Day project in the fall and was interested. However, he was occupied with a challenging position at the Alberta legislature and wasn't able to give his time to the project until after the spring election of 2012.

Exactly two weeks after the election, Gurcharan called Gurnett, took him out for a coffee and asked him to work on Daughters Day. "He didn't want to take no and I was intrigued by the project," said Gurnett. "There was just something about it."

Kirman said Daughters Day ended up being bigger than anyone had imagined. The committee held two smaller lead-up events before the Churchill Square celebration: a women's day event with an Aboriginal theme at The Carrot coffee house on 118 Avenue, and a Mother's Day event at NorQuest College that focused on South Asian women and immigrants. The group had originally planned to do four lead-up events, but found they were spending too much time on the smaller events and not enough time on the planning of the main celebration. Gurnett was concerned that the Daughters Day event might have too much of a South Asian perspective, as the main organizing committee consisted mainly of people from a South Asian background. He knew the conversations on women's issues in South Asian communities circulated around selective abortion and honour killings. However, Gurcharan and the other committee members knew they shouldn't concentrate on negative stories about women. Daughters Day needed to be a celebration and the organizers needed to acknowledge problems while celebrating the good. They tailored their activities and talks with the media accordingly.

In the early days of the project, Gurcharan wrote many letters to gather support for the event. He wrote to the United Nations and to journalist Nicholas Kristof, who had written a book on female empowerment and poverty in the developing world called *Half the Sky*. Gurcharan met with politicians to explain the project; both the city and the province offered their support. Other people assisted, but the core group did most of the work. No one knew what to expect, since Daughters Day was a new initiative. The main committee had problems with communication and decision-making. As September first approached, the group had a large amount of work to do in a short amount of time. They needed to secure the location, find speakers, arrange for food, and make sure everything else was in order. Organizers were not entirely sure that the event would be attractive to people.

Gurnett was reassured when he went to the Heritage Festival in August to hand out leaflets for Daughters Day.

He had distributed leaflets for numerous political groups and community events over the years, but people had never reacted to a flyer the way they reacted to the Daughters Day leaflets. When Gurnett gave people a flyer, he could hear them reading the message out loud and making comments as he walked away from them. They sounded excited and said they wanted to attend the event.

"I realized this was a vision of something that resonated with people," said Gurnett. He had enjoyed working on the event, but people's reactions to the leaflets made him realize Gurcharan and the other organizers had created an idea that moved people.

"One of the things I've always liked about Gurcharan, long before Daughters Day, is how totally open he is. He's a funny mix. He has absolute determination, and his own ideas about how things will be, but he is also completely non-judgmental about what happens. When things came up at meetings, like how we were forgetting the indigenous population and perspective, it just got incorporated in."

Gurcharan contributed one of the key components of the celebration- the Daughters of the Year award. The award would honour positive female role models making strong contributions to community. In 2012, the committee suggested names and tried to find four women who represented different perspectives, involvements and sectors. By 2013, the process was more formalized and there were ten categories for nomination. Creating Daughters Day was a time consuming process and the organizing committee, particularly Poushali Mitra, Paula Kirman, Charan Khehra and Gurnett worked hard over the summer months to take care of every necessary detail. Gurcharan spent hundreds of hours working on the celebration.

"I would get emails from him at five o'clock in the morning and eleven o'clock at night and everywhere in between," said Gurnett. "He's not just a guy who wants to throw ideas out to other people. He went out and did the real nuts and bolts hard work. He contacted people, talked about the event and tracked things down. He never shirks at taking on jobs. Gurcharan has a huge level of respect from people in the community and people take his requests seriously. However, there are some people who organize their lives in a way so they don't get pinned down by him and his projects."

Gurnett acknowledges that even though it isn't fair to group people, he considers Gurcharan to be part of a group of seven or eight South Asian men who came to western Canada in the 1960s and 1970s and made a significant impact. Krishan Joshee, Robinson Koilpillai and Gurcharan belong to this group, he said.

"There was something about the combination of background and personal style of these guys, the ones who came into the communities where there weren't many South Asians," he added. "These guys were themselves instead of assimilating. I don't know what it is about them, but they've been such an influence and a valuable foundation for the thousands of people who came after them. Someone has to pick up the tasks that people like Gurcharan plugged away at during all those years. We have institutions and things built into our school systems that we never would have had without these guys."

Gurnett said the men in this group have done a lot of meaningful work and influenced national policy in Canada.

"My sense is that Gurcharan loves the public attention and profile, and he finds a way to get himself to the front of so many things, but at the same time, he still does the ground work month by month by month. A guy like him deserves the front row accolades and attention because he has paid his dues every week with the unrecognized hard work."

As Daughters Day approached, some of the committee members became nervous. They had a lot of work to do and no way of knowing how the public would respond to the event. They felt there would be favourable attention, but were unsure. The committee needed a key-note speaker, and began to look for a suitable candidate. Gurcharan had admired the hard work of Karina Pillay-Kinnee during the Slave Lake forest fire in May 2011. Pillay-Kinnee was the mayor of Slave Lake, a small town of about seven thousand people, located three hours north of Edmonton. When fire threatened the entire town, all inhabitants were forced to evacuate on short notice. Dozens of homes and town build-ings, including the town hall and a newly constructed library, caught fire and burned to the ground. The fire was one of the most expensive disasters in Canadian history, with insurance claims of more than $700 million. Fortunately, no human lives were lost in the fire. Pillay-Kinnee, a three term mayor, had just turned forty years old when she became the spokesperson for her town, guiding her community calmly through the disaster and the rebuild. Gurcharan and Charan Khehra drove to Slave Lake to meet Pillay-Kinnee, who was enthusiastic about the concept of Daughters Day. She agreed to be the keynote speaker.

Committee members continued to work on the program and decided to include music, drama and dance performances as part of the event. Premier Alison Redford accepted the invitation to attend the celebration and said she would bring her daughter as well. Once Premier Redford's attendance was confirmed, Daughters Day received a great deal of me-dia attention.

On an overcast and chilly day, committee members gathered to set up rows of chairs in Churchill Square. The Daughters Day celebration began at 11 a.m. and lasted for two hours. About four hundred people came to listen to speeches and enjoy music, dancing and skits celebrating the achievements of women. The program book was filled with letters from Prime Minister Stephen Harper, Premier Redford, Mayor Stephen Mandel, city councillors, the RCMP and Alberta's New Democrat official opposition. City councillors Amarjeet Sohi, Don Iveson and Dave Loken read a scroll that proclaimed September 1, 2012 as Daughters Day in Churchill Square. Paula Kirman sang and played the Daughters Day theme song, which she had written for the event. The crowd acknowledged and celebrated the four Daughters of the Year: Karina Pillay-Kinnee, Renee Vaugeois, Faye Dewar and Rumana Monzur.

Vaugeois is the executive director of the John Humphrey Centre for Peace and Human Rights. She is also the founder of the Ainembabazi Children's Project, a charitable organization that improves the rights of orphans affected by AIDS in East Africa.

Dewar is a Métis woman who works as a health advocate at the Boyle McCauley Health Centre in an impoverished area of the inner city. She has a long record of community service in housing ventures for urban Aboriginal people, and advocacy for citizens with mental health problems. She is also an active volunteer for Aboriginal women's organizations.

Monzur was an assistant professor at Dhaka University in Bangladesh before she moved to Canada to study political science at the University of British Columbia. In June 2011, her husband attacked and blinded her during a visit to Bangladesh because she had continued her graduate studies in Canada against his wishes. Her case received widespread media attention. She returned to Vancouver in July 2011 for surgery, but the operation was unsuccessful; she was left blind in both eyes. She continues to study and raise her daughter, having left her abusive marriage.

When the crowd honoured these four remarkable women, they acknowledged the pursuit of equality for all women. Public feedback for Daughters Day was positive and all those involved with the event were pleased with the turnout and response. The organizers decided to hold Daughters Day again in 2013. Gurcharan resigned as chair, leaving the coordinator role to Gurnett. Daughters Day is expanding and has secured several sources of funding, ensuring that it will continue to grow and flourish. The province of Alberta funded public consultations with women's groups to listen to their ideas and act on them. The foundation plans to distribute a guidebook to schools, workplaces and other institutions. Gurcharan received a Man of Honour Award from the Centre to End All Sexual Exploitation (CEASE) for his effort in creating Daughters Day. He is a special Daughters Day ambassador and continues to volunteer with the group. A larger Daughters Day event was held on August 24, 2013 to bring many other community groups on board to collaborate with the original organizers. Daughters Day is another creation that is now part of one man's legacy.

E PILOGUE

Gurcharan rose early in the morning, leaving Jiti slumbering in their bed. He walked to his computer to check his e-mail and the morning news. He had articles to read and projects to consider. He read the newspaper, checked his favourite websites and then wandered down to the kitchen to make tea for his wife. Sam would come over in the early evening. He had asked his Nanni to make steak and prawns for supper.

That afternoon, Gurcharan would meet with a young journalist. The journalist had become a friend and Gurcharan had become her mentor. They spent many hours at the kitchen table together, talking about Gurcharan's life, his family and friends, and his many contributions to Canada. They discussed literature and current events while Gurcharan drank tea and the journalist sipped large glasses of water. She asked if he and Jiti had ever thought about returning to India during their first few years in Canada.

"We've been living in Canada for almost forty-eight years and we've never thought about it," said Gurcharan, looking the journalist in the eye. "Canada is home. India is the motherland, and we have friends and relatives there. Our children never think about going back to India. Our roots and projects are in Canada." He smiled. "We are happy here and proud to be Canadians."

Joe Clark and Gurcharan. Note that Joe Clark is holding a copy of *Prairie Link*.

Gurcharan, Governor General Romeo Leblanc, his wife Diane Fowler
Leblanc and Jiti. Gurcharan had just received the Order of Canada,
the highest civilian award available to a Canadian.

East West Insurance Company Visit to India. *Left to Right:* Jim Edwards,
Pritpal, Amar Singh, Dr. Manmohan Singh, Gurcharan
Bhatia, Narinder Uppal, Jarnail Sehra.

The trio responsible for the 1998 Celebration of the Universal Declaration of
Human Rights conference in Edmonton. Jack O'Neill,
Gurcharan and Gerald Gall.

Gurcharan and Jiti visiting Desmond Tutu in Capetown, South Africa,
to give him a personal invitation to the 1998 Celebration
of the Universal Declaration of Human Rights.

Judge Bhatia in his ceremonial robes, pictured with the elderly
Chinese woman who became a Canadian citizen.
She is surrounded by her family members.

CAPTION: Gurcharan with the Daughters of the Year 2012:
Left to right: Gurcharan, Renee Vaugeois, Karina Pillay-Kinnee,
Rumana Monzur and Faye Dewar.

Sam Laderoute, Priti Laderoute and Michael Laderoute.

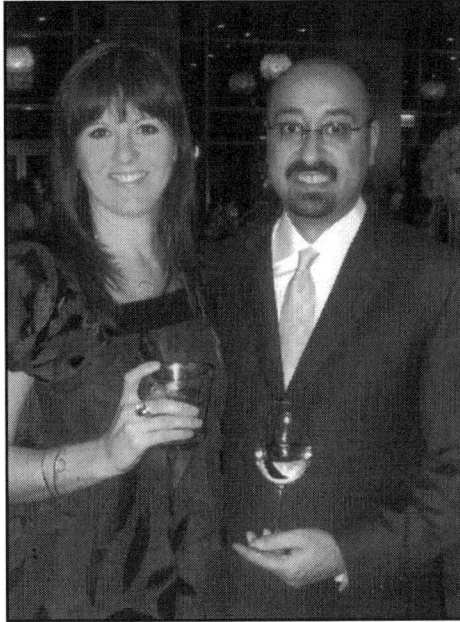

Aimee Hill and Gurvinder Bhatia.

RECOMMENDED READING

Clark, Joe *A Nation Too Good to Lose* Key Porter, 1994.

Collins, Larry and Lapierre, Dominique *Freedom at Midnight* Avon,1975.

Das, Satya *The Best Country: Why Canada will Lead the Future* Sextant, 2002.

Dickason, Olive Patricia *A Concise History of Canada's First Nations* Oxford University Press, 2006.

Frady, Marshall *Martin Luther King, A Life* Penguin, 2005.

Francis, R. Douglas; Jones, Richard; and Smith, Donald *Canadian History Since Confederation* Nelson, 2008.

Gandhi, Mohandas *The Words of Gandhi* William Morrow Books,1982.

Gandhi, Mohandas *The Story of My Experiments with Truth* Beacon Press reprint,1993.

Goyette, Linda and Roemmich, Carolina *Edmonton in Our Own Words* University of Alberta Press, 2004.

Haar, Kristen *Sikhism*, Chelsea House Publications, 2005.

Khan, Yasmin *The Great Partition* Yale University Press, 2007.

Kumar, Anu *The Mahatma and the Monkey: What Gandhiji Said and what Gandiji Did* Hachette Book Publishing, 2010.

Kissock, Heather, ed. *Protecting Rights in Canada* Weigl, 2010.

O'Connor, L.J and O'Neal, Morgan *Dark Legacy: Systemic Discrimination against Canada's First Peoples* Totem Pole Books, 2010.

Pindera, Loreen and York, Geoffery *People of the Pines* Little Brown & Company, 1991.

Satzewichm Vic *Racism in Canada* Oxford University Press, 2011.

Sparks, Allister and Mpho,Tutu *Tutu Authorized* HarperCollins, 2011.

Tutu, Desmond *God is not a Christian and other provocations* HarperOne, 2011.

Von Tunzelmann, Alex *Indian Summer* Henry Holt and Company, 2007.

About the Author

A lexis Kienlen was born in Saskatoon, Saskatchewan and currently lives in Edmonton, Alberta. She holds an International Studies degree from the University of Saskatchewan, a Graduate Diploma from Concordia University and a certificate in Food Security with a specialization in urban agriculture from Ryerson University. She has worked as a journalist since 2001. Alexis is the author of two books of poetry, *She Dreams in Red* (2007) and *13* (2011), both with Frontenac House. Her poetry, fiction and non-fiction pieces have appeared in numerous publications across Canada.

Manufactured by Amazon.ca
Bolton, ON